Bible Study for
Young Adults

POWER
Using or Abusing
Our Potential

Terri S. Cofiell

D0815764

Abingdon Press
Nashville

Power: Using or Abusing Our Potential
20/30: Bible Study for Young Adults

by Terri S. Cofiell

Scripture quotations in this publication, unless otherwise indicated, are from the New Revised Standard Version of the Bible, copyrighted © 1989 by the Division of Christian Education of the National Council of Churches of Christ in the United States of America, and are used by permission. All rights reserved.

ISBN 0-687-05217-3

This book is printed on acid-free paper.

MANUFACTURED IN THE UNITED STATES OF AMERICA.

03 04 05 06 07 08 09 10 11 12—10 9 8 7 6 5 4 3 2 1

CONTENTS

MEET THE WRITER

TERRI S. COFIELL is an ordained elder of The United Methodist Church who currently serves a congregation in Hedgesville, West Virginia. A native of Baltimore (and rampant Orioles fan), she is a graduate of Towson University in Baltimore, Maryland, and Wesley Theological Seminary in Washington, DC. Terri's ministry has included work with the Deaf community as pastor and chaplain at Magothy United Methodist Church of the Deaf, Gallaudet University, and St. Elizabeth's Hospital.

Terri and her husband, Richard Howington, share their home with their teenaged son, Zach, and two dogs, Maggie and Lulu.

WELCOME TO 20/30: BIBLE STUDY FOR YOUNG ADULTS

The *20/30* Bible study series is offered for post-modern adults who want to help structure their own discoveries—in life, in relationships, and faith. In each of the volumes of this series, you will have the opportunity to use your personal experiences in life and faith to examine the biblical texts in new ways. Each session offers biblical themes and images that have the power to shape contemporary human life.

The Power of Images

An image has evocative power. You can see, hear, smell, taste, and touch the image in your imagination. It also has the power to evoke memory and to inform ideas and feelings. Placing Christmas ornaments on a tree evokes memories of past Christmas celebrations or of circumstances surrounding the acquisition of the ornament. As an adult you may remember making the ornament as a gift for your mother, father, or another important person in your life. You may experience once again all the feelings you had when you gave this gift.

An image also informs and gives shape to themes and ideas like hope, faith, love, and compassion. The image of the ornament gives a particular shape to love because each Christmas someone carefully places it on the tree. Love becomes specific and easy to identify.

Biblical Images

The Bible offers an array of powerful and evocative images through stories, parables, poems, proverbs, and sermons. Jesus used a variety of familiar images: a woman seeking a lost coin, a merchant finding a pearl, seeds and plants, and cups that are clean on the outside but dirty on the inside. Such images transcend time and place and speak to people today. A story about a Samaritan who helped a wounded person says far more than the simple assertion that loving a neighbor means *being* a neighbor. Each of the volumes in this series connects familiar, contemporary experiences with scriptural content through a shared knowledge of theme and image.

Mystery: Experiencing the Mystery of God
Grace: Being Loved, Loving God
Balance: Living With Life's Demands
Abundance: Living Responsibly With God's Gifts
Love: Opening Your Heart to God and Others
Faith: Living a Spirited Life
Covenant: Making Commitments That Count
Exodus: Leaving Behind, Moving On
Community: Living Faithfully With Others

Experience, Faith, Growth, and Action

Each volume in this series is designed to help you explore ways in which your experience links with your faith, and how deepening your faith expands your life experiences. As a prompt for reflection, each volume has several real-life case studies. Ways to be involved in specific service opportunities are listed on pages 78-80. Activities in each session suggest ways to engage you or a group with the themes and images in the Bible.

A core Christian belief affirms that God's graceful presence and activity moves through all creation. This series is designed to support your encounters with God in a community of faith through Scripture, reflection, and dialogue. One goal of such encounters is to enhance your individual and shared commitment to serve others in the hope that they, too, might experience God's graceful presence.

HOW TO USE THIS RESOURCE

Each session of this resource includes similar components or elements:
- a statement of the issue or question to be explored
- several "voices" of persons who are currently dealing with that issue
- exploration of biblical passages relating to the question raised
- "Bible 101" boxes that provide insight about the study of the Bible
- questions for reflection and discussion
- suggested individual and group activities designed to bring the session to life
- optional case studies (found in the back of the book)
- various service learning activities related to the session (found in the back of the book)

Choices, Choices, Choices

Collectively, these components mean one thing: *choice*. You have choices to make concerning how to use each session of this resource. Want just the nitty-gritty Bible reading, reflection, and study for personal or group use? Then focus your attention on just those components during your study time. Like starting with real-life stories about issues then moving into how the Bible might be relevant? Start with the "voices" and move on from there. Use the "voices" to encourage group members to speak about their own experiences.

Prefer highly charged discussion encounters where many different viewpoints can be heard? Start the session with the biblical passages, followed by the questions and group activities. Be sure to compare the ideas found in the "Bible 101" boxes with your current ideas for more discussion. Want the major challenge of applying biblical principles to a difficult problem? After reading the biblical material, read one of the case studies, using the guidelines provided on page 14, or get involved with one of the service learning options described on pages 78-80.

Great Versatility

This resource has been designed for many different uses. Some persons will use this resource for personal study and reflection. Others will want to explore the work with a small group of friends. And still others will see this book as a different type of Sunday school resource.

Spend some time thinking about your own questions, study habits, and learning styles or those of your small group. Then use the guidelines mentioned above to fashion each session into a unique Bible study session to meet those requirements.

Highly Participatory

As you will see, the Scriptures, "voices," commentary, and experiences of group members will provide an opportunity for an active, engaging time together. The greatest challenge for a group leader might be "crowd control" —being sure everyone has the chance to put his or her ideas into the mix!

The Scriptures will help you and those who study with you to make connections between real-life issues and the Bible. This resource values and encourages personal participation as a means to understand fully and appreciate the intersection of personal belief with God's ongoing work in each and every life.

ORGANIZING A GROUP

Learning with a small group of persons offers certain advantages over studying by yourself. First, you will hopefully encounter different opinions and ideas, making the experience of Bible study a richer and more challenging event. Second, any leadership responsibilities can be shared among group members. Third, different persons will bring different talents. Some will be deep thinkers while other group members will be creative giants. Some persons will be newcomers to the Bible; their questions and comments will help others clarify their deeply held assumptions.

So how does one go about forming a small group? Follow the steps below and see how easy this task can be.

- **Read through the resource carefully.** Think about the ideas presented, the questions raised, and the exercises suggested. If the sessions of this work excite you, it will be easier for you to spread your enthusiasm to others.

- **Spend some time thinking about church members, friends, and coworkers who might find the sessions of this resource interesting**. On a sheet of paper, list two characteristics or talents you see in each person that would make him or her an attractive Bible study group member. Some talents might include "deep thinker," "creative wizard," or "committed Christian." Remember: The best small group has members who differ in learning styles, talents, ideas, and convictions, but who respect the dignity and integrity of the other members.

- **Most functional small groups have seven to fifteen members.** Make a list of potential group members that doubles your target number. For instance, if you would like a small group of seven to ten members, be prepared to invite fourteen to twenty persons.

- **Once your list of potential candidates is complete, decide on a tentative location and time.** Of course, the details can be negotiated with those persons who accept the invitation, but you need to sound definitive and clear to perspective group members. "We will initially set Wednesday night from 7 to 9 P.M. at my house for our meeting time" will sound more attractive than "Well, I don't know either when or where we would be meeting, but I hope you will consider joining us."

- **Make initial contact with prospective group members short, sweet, and to the point.** Say something like, "We are putting together a Bible study using a different kind of resource. When would be a good time to show you the resource and talk about the study?" Establishing a special time to make the invitation takes the pressure off the prospective group member to make a quick decision.

- **Show up at the decided time and place.** Talk with each prospective member individually. Bring a copy of the resource with you. Show each person what excites you about the study and mention the two unique characteristics or talents you feel he or she would offer the group. Tell each person the initial meeting time and location and how many weeks the small group will meet. Also mention that the need for a new time or location could be discussed during the first group meeting. Ask for a commitment to come to the first session. Thank each person for his or her time.

- **Give a quick phone call or e-mail to thank all persons for their consideration and interest.** Remind persons of the time and location of the first meeting.

- **Be organized.** Use the first group meeting to get acquainted. Briefly describe the seven sessions. Have a book for each group member, and discuss sharing responsibilities for leadership.

PREPARING TO LEAD

So the responsibility to lead the group has fallen upon you? Don't sweat it. Follow these simple suggestions and you will not only prepare to lead you will also find that your mind and heart are open to encounter the Christ who is with you.

- **Pray.** Find a quiet place. Have your Bible, the *20/30* book, paper, and pen handy. Ask for God's guidance and inspiration as you prepare for the session.

- **Read.** Look up all the Bible passages. Take careful notes about the ideas, statements, questions, and activities in the session. Jot down ideas and insights that occur to you as you read.

- **Think about group members.** Which ones like to think about ideas, concepts, or problems? Which ones need to "feel into" an idea by storytelling, worship, prayer, or group activities? Which ones are the "actors" who prefer a hands-on or participatory approach? Which ones might help you lead the session? Pray for each of the persons.

- **Think about the learning area and supplies.** What might you do with the place where you meet in order to enhance the experiences and activities of the session? Make a list of things like poster paper, pens or pencils, paper, markers, large white paper, supplies for more creative activities, Bibles, music, hymnals, or any other supplies you might need for the activities in the session.

- **Think about special arrangements.** You may need to make special arrangements: inviting a guest speaker, planning an activity that occurs outside the regular time and place, or acquiring audio-visual equipment, for example.

- **Pray.** After you have thought through all the steps listed above, thank God for insights and inspiration about leading the group.

Using the Activity Icons

20/30 volumes include activity boxes marked with icons or images that indicate the kind of activity described in the box. The icons are intended to help you make decisions about which activities will best meet the needs of your group.

Start. A get-acquainted activity that introduces the focus of the session.

 Discuss. Activities designed to stimulate large group discussion.

 Small Group. Activities designed to stimulate discussion and reflection in groups of two or three persons. See the section "Using Break-out Groups" on pages 15-16.

 Bible. A Bible study activity that lists specific Scriptures. Participants will use the Bible.

 Look Closer. An activity designed to promote deeper, reflective awareness for an individual or for a group. The activity may call for use of resources like Bible dictionaries or commentaries.

 Create. An activity designed for using a variety of creative art forms: drawing, sculpting, creating a mobile or a collage, or writing a poem or story.

 Case Study. An activity designed to explore and discuss a unique case study related to the session content or one of the case studies included in the back of the book.

 Serve. An activity that invites the group to discuss and engage in service to others. May relate directly to session content or to one of the service options in the back of the book.

 Music. An activity that uses music. May invite listening to a CD or singing a hymn, for example.

 Close. A closing activity that invites worship, celebration, or commitment to some specific action as a result of experiencing the session.

CHOOSING TEACHING OPTIONS

This young adult series was designed, written, and produced out of an understanding of the attributes, concerns, joys, and faith issues of young adults. With great care and integrity, this image-based print resource was developed to connect biblical events and relationships with contemporary, real-life situations of young adults. Its pages will promote Christian relationships and community, support new biblical learning, encourage spiritual development, and empower faithful decision-making and action.

This study is well-suited to young adults and may be used confidently and effectively. But with the great diversity within the young adult population, not every line of this study will be written "just for you." To be most relevant, some portions of the study material need to be tailored to fit your particular group. Adjustments for a good fit involve making choices from options offered by the resource. This customizing may be done easily by a designated leader who is familiar with the layout of the resource and the young adults who are using it.

What to Expect

In this study Scripture and real-life images mesh together to provoke a personal response. Young adults will find themselves thinking, feeling, imagining, questioning, making decisions, professing faith, building connections, inviting discipleship, taking action, and making a difference. Scripture is at the core of each session. Scenarios weave in the dimensions of real life. Narrative and text boxes frame plenty of teaching options to offer young adults.

Each session is part of a cohesive volume, but it is also designed to stand alone. One session is not dependent on knowledge or experience accumulated from other sessions. A group leader can freely choose from the teaching options in an individual session without wondering about how it might affect the other sessions.

A Good Fit

For a better fit, alter the session based on what is known about the young adult participants. Young adults are a diverse constituency with varied experiences, interests, needs, and values. There is really no single defining characteristic that links young adults. Specific information about the age, employment status, household, personal relationships, and lifestyle among participants will equip a leader to make choices that ensure a good fit.

- **Customize.** Read through the session. Notice how scenarios and teaching options move from integrating Scripture and real-life dimensions to inviting a response.

- **Look at the scenario(s).** How real is the presentation of real life? Say that the main character is a professional, white male, married, in his early twenties, and caught in a workplace dilemma that entangles his immediate superior and a subordinate from his division. Perhaps your group members are mostly college students and recent graduates, unmarried, and still on the way to being "settled." There are many differences between the man in the scenario and these group members.

  As a leader you could choose to eliminate the case study, substitute it with another scenario (there are several more choices on pages 75-77), claim the validity of the dilemma and shift the spotlight from the main character to the subordinate, or modify the description of the main character. Break-out groups based on age or employment experience might also be used to accommodate the differences and offer a better fit.

- **Look at the teaching options.** How are the activities propelling participants toward a personal response? Perhaps the Scripture study requires more meditative quiet than is possible and a more academic, verbal, or artistic approach would offer a better fit. Maybe more direct decisions or actions would fit better than more passive or logical means. Try to keep a balance, though, that allows participants to "get out of their head" to reflect and also to move toward action.

  Conceivably, there could be too much in any one session. As a leader, you can pick and choose among teaching options, substitute case studies, take two meetings to do one session, and adapt any process to make a better fit. The tailoring process can be evaluated as adjustments are made. Judge the fit every time you meet. Ask questions that gauge relevance, and assess how the resource has stretched minds, encouraged discipleship, and changed lives.

USING BREAK-OUT GROUPS

20/30 break-out groups are small groups that encourage the personal sharing of lives and the gospel. The word *break-out* is a sweeping term that includes a variety of small group settings. A break-out group may resemble a Bible study group, an interest group, a sharing group, or other types of Christian fellowship groups.

Break-out groups offer young adults a chance to belong and personally relate to one another. Members are known, nurtured, and heard by others. Young adults may agree and disagree while maximizing the exchange of ideas, information, or options. They might explore, confront, and resolve personal issues and feelings with empathy and support. Participants can challenge and hold each other accountable to a personalized faith and stretch the break-out group's links to real life and service.

Forming Break-out Groups

As you look through this book, you will see an icon that says "small group." The nature of these small break-out groups will depend on the context and design of the specific session. On occasion the total group of participants will be divided for a particular activity. Break-out groups will differ from one session to the next. Variations may involve the size of the group, how group members are divided, or the task of the group. Break-out groups may also be used to accommodate differences and help tailor the session plan for a better fit. In some sessions, specific group assembly instructions will be provided. For other sessions, decisions regarding the size or division of small groups will be made by the designated leader. Break-out groups may be in the form of pairs or trios, family-sized groups of three to six members, or groups of up to ten members.

They may be arranged simply by grouping persons seated next to one another or in more intentional ways by common interests, characteristics, or life experience. Consider creating break-out groups according to age; gender; type of household, living arrangements, or love relationships; vocation, occupation, career, or employment status; common or built-in connections; lifestyle; values or perspective; or personal interests or traits.

Membership

The membership of break-out groups will vary from session to session, or even within specific sessions. Young adults need to work at knowing and being known, so that there can be a balance between break-out groups that are more similar and those that reflect greater diversity. There may be times when more honest communication, trust, or accountability may be desired and group leaders will need to be free to self-select members for small groups.

It is important for *20/30* break-out groups to practice acceptance and to value the worth of others. The potential for small groups to encourage personal sharing and significant relationships is enhanced when members agree to exercise active listening skills, keep confidences, expect authenticity, foster trust, and develop ways of loving one another. All group members contribute to the development and function of break-out groups. Designated leaders especially need to model manners of hospitality and help ensure that each group member is respected.

Invitational Listening

Consider establishing an "invitational listening" routine that validates the perspective and affirms the voice of each group member. After a question or statement is posed, pause and allow time to think—not all persons think on their feet or talk out loud to think. Then, initiate conversation by inviting one group member, by name, to talk. This person may either choose to talk or to "pass." Either way, this person is honored and is offered an opportunity to speak and to be heard. This person carries on the ritual by inviting another group member, by name, to speak. The process continues until all have been invited, by name, to talk. As each one invites another, the responsibility of acceptance and hospitality in the break-out groups is shared among all its members.

Study group members break-out to belong, to share the gospel, to care, and to watch over one another in Christian love. "So deeply do we care for you that we are determined to share with you not only the gospel of God but also our own selves, because you have become very dear to us" (1 Thessalonians 2:8).

POWER:
USING OR ABUSING OUR POTENTIAL

"I've got the power." The line from the song echoed in Carlos's mind. It seemed to him that these words had become a sort of manifesto for the new millennium. *Let's face it,* he thought. *While we'd hate to be labeled "power hungry," we are inundated with ways of appeasing the appetite. Power abounds. We wake up, go for a power walk or pop in a power aerobics video, grab a power bar on the way to our power shower, and power dress ourselves. Don't forget that power tie, guys—red in the Eighties, yellow in the Nineties, purple for the time being—all before hitting work. Then there's the power lunch with the power brokers followed by the power nap, the power plays, the powering down for our return home. Why, then, do so many people feel so powerless? Powerless in the marketplace. Powerless in the political order. Powerless in relationships. Powerless against crime or against terrorism.*

Power can be so elusive. Finding, gaining, claiming, and retaining power have become fodder for countless books and TV talk shows, as well as corporate seminars and personal growth retreats. A search on the Internet will yield hits for personal coaches and life strategists for those in need of one-on-one professional assistance in attaining power for career or personal enhancement. Empowerment, it would seem, is becoming an industry in America.

The demand for power of a more tangible variety is on the rise as well. According to the US Department of Energy, domestic power consumption has nearly tripled between 1950 and 2000, with an anticipated increase of 32 percent by the year 2020. Meanwhile, British researchers are busy developing the ultimate in power suits—clothing that will use body heat to power cell phones, hand-held computers, and all the assorted accoutrements of life in a high-powered world. Like the fictional Toolman of the popular Nineties sitcom, we know what we need: "More power!" For our cars and computers, our microwave ovens and video game systems, we know what we want: "More power!" To climb the ladder of success, to win at love or war, to satisfy our craving for energy and security, the answer is clear: "More power!" So how do we get it?

Establishing a Power Base

If you're a toaster, accessing power is a relatively straightforward procedure. Once you've been plugged in, assuming the electric bill has been paid and the fossil fuels hold out, you're set to make toast. For human beings

---

things are a bit more complicated. Think of the most powerful people you know from history, media, or personal experience. What was the source of their power? Was it birthright, wealth, physical or military superiority, celebrity, influence, or something else? What kind of power did they wield?

During the 1960's and 1970's, coalitions formed within communities and constituencies whose members were among the disenfranchised—the least powerful—segments of American society. These power-to-the-people movements challenged the existing powers. "One man's hands can't tear a prison down," the old protest song proclaimed. "But when two and two and fifty make a million, we'll see that day come 'round." Black Power, Red Power, and Flower Power were the rallying cries of those whose mission was nothing less than to change the world. The term *power base* first appeared in *The Merriam-Webster Dictionary* in 1959, but the idea has been around for a very long time. Think of Gandhi, the Suffragettes, Moses and the Hebrew slaves, any number of revolutions in any number of places, those who reclaimed power in their worlds by uniting for a common purpose.

Plugging Into the Power Source

Human beings, whether individually or collectively, do have one thing in common with the aforementioned toaster: Their power is always derived from a source. Robert Greene and Joost Elffers examine the tactics of notable power players throughout history in their book, *The 48 Laws of Power*. Using insights from the likes of Machiavelli and Alexander the Great, they distill a set of rules for winning the power game, including Law 15, "Crush your enemy totally"; Law 33, "Discover each man's thumbscrew"; and, borrowing from the prophet Zechariah (as quoted by Jesus), Law 42, "Strike the shepherd and the sheep will scatter." Can power be obtained only through domination or manipulation? As followers of the Shepherd we would be hard pressed to agree; yet we find ourselves enmeshed in a world where keeping the upper hand is not merely affirmed but applauded. Can we survive in a me-first world and remain faithful to the One who said, "Whoever wants to be first must be last of all and servant of all?" (Mark 9:35b).

This volume will explore power as it is understood, experienced, used, and all too often abused in secular society, in the church, and in the Bible itself. Through Bible study, discussion, and reflection we'll trace our personal "power cables" back to their Source. We'll even tackle the "V word," vulnerability, as we share what it means to be open to God and to one another. Remember: We've got the power! As Paul wrote to Timothy: "God did not give us a spirit of cowardice, but rather a spirit of power and of love and of self-discipline" (2 Timothy 1:7).

POWER, POWER EVERYWHERE BUT . . .

This session will introduce and define *power* as it is encountered in human experience and biblical witness.

GETTING STARTED

Who was your favorite superhero when you were a kid? Did you ever dress as a Ninja Turtle for Halloween or run through the house with a terry cloth cape tied around your neck? Who wouldn't want to be Batman, Wonder Woman, or a Power Ranger? It's not a bad gig. You get superhuman powers, a really cool costume, and—best of all—you get to win in the end. Bad people always get what's coming to them.

Then you grow up. You trade in your tights and cape for a pinstripe power suit, a hardhat, or scrubs. You learn that nice people do, all too often, finish last. You quickly discover that your "powers" are very human and very limited. But the power is out there, or so they say. Corporate trainers write bestselling

Introduce yourselves by telling your name and completing the sentence "Power means _____." Look at magazine or newspaper images that suggest power. How do the images suggest power?

Brainstorm a list of powerful people from the past and present. What is the source of their power? Who do you see as most powerful? Why?

Coming to Terms With Power
How would you define *power* in marriage? friendships? work? international events? the economy? other? How do you think power in such situations affects a person's sense of personal power? What situations do you think make a person feel most powerful? least powerful? Why?

how-to manuals for seizing power. Motivational speakers, self-help gurus, and even preachers try to persuade you that power is yours for the claiming. Singers go platinum promoting the notion that "the hero lies in you." If only you could tap into the source!

COMING TO TERMS WITH POWER

Perhaps power seems so elusive because *power* is so hard to define. *The Merriam-Webster Dictionary* lists no fewer than 39 entries for *power*. Several are very concrete: *power* as a source for supplying energy, *power* as magnification, *power* as a factor in multiplication. *Power* as an attribute of humans, systems, or even things, however, is a little harder to grasp.

Which is more powerful, a six-pound, seven-ounce newborn baby or a 330-pound offensive lineman in the NFL? If you're talking *power* as physical superiority, it's a no-brainer. But the cry of that tiny, fragile infant has the power to bring people

SMALL GROUP

No-Win Power Game
Form groups of three, and play a few rounds of "Paper, Scissors, Rock." How are the power principles of this children's game lived out in the adult world?

more than twenty times her size running. Her smile has the power to melt the heart of that 330-pound offensive lineman. There's more to power than meets the eye.

Power as influence, *power* as control, *power* as authority, *power* as the "ability to act or produce an effect"; the list goes on and on. Most of us have been on the giving as well as the receiving ends of influence, control, or authority. We may not be able to control what the networks broadcast, but we have the power to turn off the TV, install a V-Chip, or monitor our children's viewing if we find the programming objectionable. We can use our power as consumers to influence the advertisers who pay for these shows by boycotting their products—just as we can use our voting power to lobby against censorship in the media.

Individually we may have little influence in the political process, but if we use the influence we have among our friends and neighbors, they may sign a petition that will influence the voting of our elected officials. If those who sign our petition begin to collect signatures within their own circles of influence, our power base can expand to the "nth" power!

A NO-WIN POWER GAME

An old Simon and Garfunkel tune said, "I'd rather be a hammer than a nail"; but in reality the sentiments expressed by other musicians illustrate the greater truth: "Sometimes you're the windshield; sometimes you're the bug." Our personal power is often relative to the situation in which we find ourselves, just as the degree of our power is relative to how we put that power to use. Remember the little Dutch kid

In Other Words . . .
Look in a thesaurus or dictionary to find synonyms related to power. Make a list of these synonyms on a large sheet of white paper. As a group decide if each word has a positive (+), negative (-), or neutral (0) connotation. Are there more positive, negative, or neutral images? What about power itself? Is power positive or negative--good or bad? How does the use or abuse of power affect your understanding of power as either negative or positive?

who used his finger to plug a leak in the dike? The people of Haarlem in the Netherlands remember. They erected a monument to him.

IN OTHER WORDS . . .

Perhaps *power* is best defined as it is applied in specific situations. To say that a person is "controlling" is hardly complimentary, and to say that he or she is "out of control" is no less flattering. *Sovereignty, dominion, oppression, coercion, sway.* Each of these concepts is related to power, yet the connotation is different for each. Being "under the authority" of our employer or supervisor is hardly the same as being "under the boss's thumb."

Fire is a powerful thing; it can warm our hands on a cold night and our hearts as we snuggle in front of the hearth. It can refine precious metals, barbecue steaks, drive a car, or light up a birthday cake. At Pentecost the power of the Holy Spirit was manifest in "divided tongues, as of fire" (Acts 2:3) that rested on each of the disciples. Fire can also destroy a home, ravage a forest, ignite a cross, or disfigure a child.

Water has the power to put out a fire; it can also sustain a life, bathe a baby, sink a ship, or drown a swimmer. Biblical water had the power to wipe out an unfaithful people or wash away a people's sins. The same dichotomy extends to human endeavors. A jetliner has the power to defy gravity. In the hands of a trained pilot, it can safely transport hundreds of people. In the hands of a

In Biblical Terms
Choose a timekeeper. Working together, list as many powerful people/entities from Scripture as you can in one minute. As a group, decide upon the five most powerful, ranking them in descending order. What was the source of power for each? Was that power from God? Was it used for or against God?

Take another minute to list as many powerful acts/events as you can think of from the Old and New Testaments. Again, rate your top five answers. Were all five "acts of God"? In which acts was God's power demonstrated in ways you find destructive or unsettling? How are these actions congruent or incongruent with the image of a loving, creative God?

Look up *powers* in a Bible dictionary. Also look at notes in your Bible for the following verses: Isaiah 24:21; Daniel 4:35; Romans 8:38; and 1 Peter 3:22. How do you understand the kinds of power suggested by "host of heaven," "angels," or "demons" in the Bible? How does your understanding compare or contrast with biblical expressions of spiritual powers?

Power: Using or Abusing Our Potential

terrorist, it can become a guided missile.

The power of love, the power of the press, the power of prayer, the power of celebrity, the power of positive thinking. How is each measured? Political power, military power, economic power, technological power. Might does not always make right. Power is best understood and judged as it is used or abused.

IN BIBLICAL TERMS

If you think the dictionary has a lot of listings for *power,* try a concordance. Depending on the version of Scripture you're using, you will find more than 350 entries (not to mention words like *dominion, rule,* and *reign).* Almost every use and abuse of power you can think of is illustrated in the Bible. It's all in there: the cosmic battle between good and evil, the wealth of nations, the thrill of victory, the agony of defeat.

In the Hebrew Bible, which Christians call the Old Testament, no less than a dozen Hebrew words are translated "power." The meanings include such concepts as vigor, firmness, ability, dominion, strength, boldness, ability to resist, endure, prevail, overcome, force, valor, wealth, authority, and mastery. The Hebrew word *yad* suggests the power of an open hand and includes "service"

The First Power Struggle
Divide the first three chapters of Genesis among three small groups. Identify the images or acts of power in your chapter, and jot down a name for each. Bring the groups together.

Look at each character in the Creation narrative: God, Adam, Eve, the serpent. How would you characterize the power of each? Which do you see as most powerful? least powerful? Why?

How do you understand dominion? What do you think it means for humankind to "have dominion over the fish of the sea and over the birds of the air and over every living thing that moves upon the earth"? (Genesis 1:28). Does *dominion* have a positive, negative, or neutral connotation for you? What similarities or differences do you see between *dominion* and *domination*?

The Balance of Power
Edward Bulwer-Lytton is credited with coining the phrase "The pen is mightier than the sword," a 19th century adaptation of a 16th century proverb. Using a show-of-hands vote, determine which of the following concepts in each pair tips the power scales for you.

Which is more powerful?
• words or weapons
• water or stone
• love or hate
• forgiveness or vengeance
• greed or generosity
• ideals or actions
• popularity or self-respect
• prejudice or acceptance
• good or evil

Do you think you would have voted differently in a different context (if you weren't in church) or at a different age? How would your perspective change in different situations? How is your understanding of what is powerful related to values and beliefs?

among its meanings. In the New Testament, the words *dunamis* and *exousia* are used most often. *Dunamis* carries the sense of "force," which is often understood as miraculous power. It also means ability, abundance, and strength. *Exousia* points more to ability, competency, capacity, and mastery. It also suggests freedom, right, and liberty.

THE FIRST POWER STRUGGLE

From page one, the Bible is about power: God says, and it's so. Flip ahead a page or two, and the power struggle begins. The one thing the humans are not supposed to do is the very thing they can't resist doing. "See," God says, "the man has become like one of us" (Genesis 3:22). It's not that humans are powerless; it's how they use the power they are given that gets them into trouble.

A good example is Samson. Like superheroes in comic books, Samson was endowed by God with superhuman physical power. When the wily Delilah learned the source of his strength—"If my head were shaved, then my strength would leave me; I would become weak, and be like anyone else" (Judges 16:17)—she quickly called for a barber. His power vanished; his enemies easily subdued him. However, Samson confused the source of his power with the sign of his vow. As a Nazirite, he was prohibited from shaving his head. The razor, however, was not a form of divine kryptonite, but a failure of faithfulness that proved to be Samson's undoing. Samson forgot that God was the source of his

BIBLE

Samson
Working in four groups, read one chapter each from Judges 13-16. List the uses and abuses of power in your chapter. Repeat your findings to the entire group. In the large group review the story of Samson and the material in "Bible 101." How would you characterize Samson? Other than physical ability, do you see any strengths in Samson? What are his weaknesses? How does he abuse his power and position?

What does the story say to you about God's faithfulness to Samson? about the nature of God? about power?

strength. He forgot who was really in control.

A BALANCE OF POWER

This debate over who's in charge will continue until, like Jesus said, "You do not know when the time will come" (Mark 13:33). Human beings have long struggled against the limitations to their power, often to the benefit of humankind. By harnessing the powers of fire, water, and electricity, life-affirming strides have been made in science, technology, and medicine.

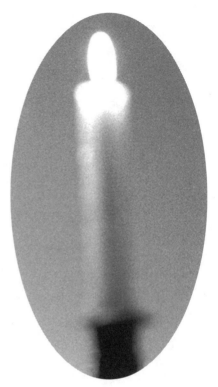

These very same powers have also been used to destroy life. The same virus isolated to develop a vaccine can be used as a biological weapon. Too often, humans choose to use their power against one another. Oppression is alive and thriving in the 21st century.

The challenge for God's people in any age remains the same: How do we claim and use our God-given power without succumbing to the temptation to abuse it? How do we find balance? Remembering who we are in relationship to God and to one another is a good place to start. God created us. God loves us. God gave us power. God calls us to use our power for the growth of mercy, justice, and compassion in all of our relationships, with one another and with creation. The key is staying plugged in to the right power Source.

CLOSE

Find a partner and talk about a place in your life where you feel powerless. Pray together for empowerment by the Holy Spirit to live your discipleship boldly. Covenant to pray for each other throughout the coming week.

I AM WEAK, BUT THOU ART STRONG

This session will explore the themes of powerlessness, weakness, and vulnerability.

GETTING STARTED

Would you try a new deodorant if the makers claimed it was weaker than their original formula? Does anyone aspire to reach the bottom of the heap? Probably not. Society and survival have taught us to keep our vulnerabilities well under wraps and to "never let them see you sweat." Jesus teaches something a little different: "Blessed are the meek, for they will inherit the earth" (Matthew 5:5). So does the apostle Paul: "God chose what is foolish in the world to shame the wise; God chose what is weak in the world to shame the strong" (1 Corinthians 1:27).

THE WEAKEST LINK

The old saying, "a chain is only as strong as its weakest link," has found new meaning in popular culture. Some of the highest rated television game shows of recent years have put this proverb to the test, requiring that contestants not only strategize, but *survive* in order to win. Just how

Check in with one another and introduce yourselves to any newcomers. Sing "Jesus Loves Me" together. Tell about your earliest memories of this song. What did it mean to you as a child to sing, "Little ones to him belong; they are weak, but he is strong"? What do those words mean to you now?

Do you see *weak* as having any positive connotations? Do you see a difference between being meek and being weak? How would you feel about being called meek? Would you feel particularly blessed? Why or why not?

do you survive? In large part by exploiting your opponents' weaknesses and allying with others to pick them off one by one. From the gladiators of ancient Rome to *The WWF*, contests based on the total annihilation of the opposition have been crowd pleasers. Look at our idioms; the English language is full of "weakest link" metaphors. Want to overcome your enemy? Look for the *chink in his armor*, search out her *Achilles' heel*, expose the soft underbelly, go for the jugular, hit 'em where it hurts; and when you stick the knife in, twist it!

GOD CHOSE WHAT IS WEAK

Paul challenged the forming of alliances in his first letter to the church in Corinth. Corinth, at the time of Paul's letter, was a thriving, cosmopolitan center of trade and learning with a multiethnic population. In many ways ancient Corinth has much in common with modern American society. Factions of believers were gathering around certain leaders and their teachings. Since the New Testament was not yet written, there was not a standard recorded witness concerning Jesus at the time. "Has Christ been divided? Was Paul crucified for you?" (1 Corinthians 1:13). Paul reminded the Corinthians that he was sent "to proclaim the gospel" (verse 17). He also reminded them that God called and equipped the Corinthian Christians. "Let the one who boasts, boast in the Lord" (verse 31).

Should the Corinthians be tempted to boast in *their* accomplishments, in the excellence of *their* knowledge and speech, Paul provided the ultimate in reality checks:

"God's foolishness is wiser than human wisdom, and God's weakness is stronger than human strength" (verse 25). The biblical evidence is overwhelming. From Genesis to Revelation, God repeatedly chooses highly unlikely instruments to bring about God's purposes and to confound human logic. Demonstrations of this are seen in Jesus' crucifixion.

God Chose What Is Weak
Form groups of two or three. Choose from the following Scriptures. Read your passage and any accompanying annotations, and discuss the following: Who are the actors in each scene? What do you know about their place in the society of their day? What do you learn about God from each of these stories? How does God use what the world considers weak to shame what the world considers powerful?

Judges 4
1 Samuel 17:1-51
Matthew 5:1-12
Matthew 9:35-38
Mark 12:38-44

Luke 2:8-20
Luke 18:1-8
Luke 18:9-14
Luke 18:15-17

CROSS PURPOSES

Some of you may wear or own cross jewelry. You may have received a cross pendant as a gift to commemorate a special occasion like baptism or confirmation. The cross may be a special treasure to you.

In the ancient world, a cross had very different meanings. A crucifixion implied far more than punishment for a capital offense; the cross, in the words of first-century historian Josephus, represented "the most wretched of deaths." Reserved for members of the lowest classes of society, crucifixion was a public spectacle of humiliation—a painful and prolonged struggle against exposure and asphyxiation. It was an act of state terror used to intimidate and to keep the masses in submission. The word *cross* itself was not spoken in polite society.

For those who don't know Christ, the cross is "foolishness" and a "stumbling block" and the ultimate sign of Rome's power over conquered people. Perhaps that is why the extent of God's power is most evident in Jesus' vulnerability: "For this reason the Father loves me, because I lay down my life in order to take it

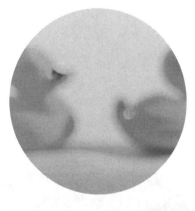

Look Closer
Read the first chapter of First Corinthians and any accompanying introductory material or annotations in your Bible. Do you see any similarities to contemporary American society when it comes to divisions within the body of Christ—the church? What factions do you see within Christianity? within individual congregations?

up again. No one takes it from me, but I lay it down of my own accord. I have power to lay it down, and I have power to take it up again" (John 10:17-18a).

While Jews were accustomed to and comfortable with the concept of sacrifice, crucifixion was particularly abhorrent in light of God's own law: "For anyone hung on a tree is under God's curse" (Deuteronomy 21:23). A crucified Savior was unthinkable. The Messiah of Israel's longing would certainly be a conqueror. In the line of David, God's Anointed One was expected to live up to David's image. The Jews were looking for a warrior king, not a sacrifice.

WHAT'S IN A NAME?

As power was conveyed through names in Jewish antiquity, so power is conveyed in the New Testament proclamation through the titles conferred upon Jesus. This power, though, is often easier to understand in the Jesus we affirm as fully divine, the King of kings and Lord of lords. It's the fully human

Bible 101: The Lamb of God
John's Gospel is filled with declarations concerning Jesus. Jesus is the Word, the light of the world, God incarnate. Upon his first encounter with Jesus, John proclaimed, "Here is the Lamb of God who takes away the sin of the world!" (John 1:29). The image recalls the paschal lamb of the Jewish Passover and the last of God's plagues when the first-born of Egypt were slain while the children of Israel were spared. Elaborate preparations for the lamb are specified in Exodus 12, including the marking of the doorposts with lamb's blood: "When I see the blood, I will pass over you" (Exodus 12:13).

The Hebrew children were saved through the blood of the lamb, just as the post-Resurrection community understands that its own salvation is secured through "the precious blood of Christ, like that of a lamb without defect or blemish" (1 Peter 1:19). Isaiah 53:1-12, one of the suffering servant songs, is commonly interpreted by Christians as a prophecy concerning Jesus. Revelation 5:1-13 is part of an apocalyptic vision given to John concerning the final triumph of God's righteousness. Both these forms of writing are unfamiliar to many modern readers, yet both focus on the image of God's Lamb.

aspect of Jesus' nature that gives us pause, perhaps because it highlights our own sense of personal vulnerability.

We have imposed an emotional, relational connotation on the word *vulnerable*; but in reality it simply means to be "capable of being physically wounded" or "open to attack or damage." While this seems to us a risky business, it is precisely through Jesus' death and resurrection that death itself is overcome. More than that, Jesus called his followers to share in that vulnerability, to turn the other cheek (Matthew 5:39), to go the extra mile (5:41), to pick up their crosses and follow him (16:24). He sent the Twelve into the world as sheep among wolves (10:16).

Jesus' teachings about vulnerability taught the people how to survive when under the control of an arbitrary and capricious tyrant. To strike back when slapped by a soldier invited death. Not to carry a soldier's pack was a risk. Carrying it the extra distance would help demonstrate that the one carrying it was not anti-Roman. Such vulnerability gave the power of choice to an oppressed people.

What's in a Name?
Read the titles and roles of Jesus listed below. Working individually, rate these images from most powerful (15) to least powerful (1). Come together and compare your lists. Are they similar? different? Did you have trouble deciding? Can you think of any other titles for Jesus? How would you rate them?

Which of these images is most comfortable for you? Which is least comfortable? Why?

Miracle Worker
Redeemer
Prince of Peace
Lamb of God
Bread of Life
Healer
Suffering Servant

Exorcist
Wonderful Counselor
Sacrifice
Messiah
Christ
Good Shepherd
The Word
Teacher

SHEEP AMONG WOLVES

Who wants to be a sheep among wolves? How do we live out a call that flies in the face of all contemporary society teaches us about self preservation? Jesus taught self-preservation in a different culture. He said, "See, I am sending you out like sheep into the midst of wolves; so be wise as serpents and innocent as doves" (Matthew 10:16). Don't challenge authority when it will get you killed. As a sheep among wolves, you can lay low and survive.

PAUL BOASTED OF WEAKNESS

Paul spoke about weakness and power in a different context. As he addressed controversy involving opponents in the church at Corinth and a different gospel than the one proclaimed by Paul, he employed a fierce irony about boasting: "If I must boast, I will boast of the things that show my weakness" (2 Corinthians 11:30). The irony of his argument serves to show Paul's true power, a power derived from Christ: "He said to me, 'My grace is sufficient for you, for power is made perfect in weakness.' So, I will boast all the more gladly of my weaknesses, so that the power of Christ may dwell in me. Therefore I am content with weaknesses, insults, hardships, persecutions, and calamities for the sake of Christ; for whenever I am weak, then I am strong" (12:9-10).

Instead of denying our weaknesses, foibles, and failures, we can look at them objectively and learn from them. They may well lead us to deeper reservoirs of power. As Paul boasted of his weaknesses, it is quite clear that he was strong in the power of Christ. When we become aware of our weaknesses, we also become aware of our need for God.

CASE STUDY
The Stumbling Block

Randall was used to jokes aimed at short people. He had heard them all his life. His mother had always promised, "One day you'll catch up." But at 32, it seemed that

5'5," 135 pounds was as caught up as he was ever going to be. On the whole, life was good: a beautiful 5'1" wife, two great kids, a house, and a job that he loved. Then Bob moved into the cubicle next to Randall at the office—foul mouthed, obnoxious, 6'3" Bob.

From day one Bob had referred to Randall as "Junior." He even had the gall to ask if he needed a booster seat to reach his keyboard! Suddenly Randall felt 14 again, and it was getting worse by the day.

At first he tried to be a good sport and to play along with Bob's insults. When he finally asked Bob to call him Randall, Bob just patted him on the head. Randall told his wife he was thinking about looking for a new job, and she suggested he talk with his supervisor. "Oh, that'll really be great. Our new supervisor is a 26-year-old woman. Let her fight my battles, right? I can just hear Bob now."

The New Kid on the Block

Izzie had finished off two bottles of antacid in the past week. Her department was behind for the quarter, and her boss had been pressing her for results. "When we made you supervisor, we had every confidence that you could get the job done. You've got to get tough with these people. We need to see some results."

Izzie didn't feel very tough. She had worked so hard to get this promotion, and she deserved it. She had been her department's number one producer for two years straight. When she worked in the main office, she had always felt respected by her coworkers (well, except for that idiot Bob); but once they had to answer to her, things changed. She had always believed that "you

Lamb of God
Play a quick game of word association with the word *lamb*. What is the first word or image that comes to mind?

Working in two groups, read Isaiah 53:1-12 and Revelation 5:1. Compare these images of the Lamb. What does the image of God's Lamb suggest to you? Do you see power in Christ's vulnerability? Explain your answer.

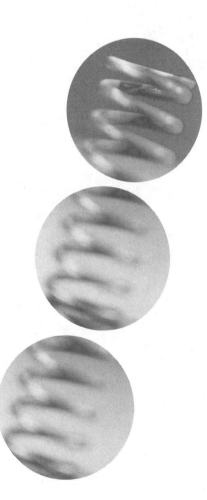

I Am Weak, But Thou Art Strong

Sheep Among Wolves
In groups of two or three, spend a few minutes brainstorming modern parallels to the image of "a sheep among wolves." Have you ever felt this vulnerable, this open to attack? In what situations? How did you respond? If you could replay those scenes, would you do anything differently?

What, if anything, can we learn from our weaknesses and shortcomings? How might we use our weakness to help others? to serve God?

Case Studies
Working in three groups, read the "The Stumbling Block," "The New Kid on the Block," and "A Chip Off the Old Block" on pages 32-34. Discuss the following for your group's character: Why does he or she feel powerless or ineffectual? What is the source of these feelings? What would it take to change the balance of power in the situation?

How do you see the role of upper level management in each case? What connections do you make between the biblical discussions of weakness, vulnerability, and power and each of these case studies?

Form groups of two or three and read Romans 8:26 aloud in unison. Tell about situations in your life that leave you feeling vulnerable or unable to act decisively. After each person speaks, read the verse aloud again, then pray silently together.

can catch more flies with honey than vinegar," but it didn't seem to be working. Now she found herself working even harder to take up some of their slack.

So far, her only executive action had been to move Bob into her old cubicle—as far from her new office as possible. If he weren't so good at his job, she would get rid of him; but at least now she didn't have to listen to his disgusting comments all day.

A Chip Off the Old Block

"Well, Bob, I guess it's up to me to call since you're obviously too busy to pick up a phone."

"Sorry, Dad; I've been meaning to—"

"I guess that supervisor's job has been keeping your nose to the grindstone, eh?"

"Not exactly. I didn't get it, Dad. You know how it is. I'm the wrong sex and the wrong color. They gave it to some girl who'd been here half as long as I have."

"Maybe if you had stayed in college you could have made something of yourself. Look at your brother: He had his MBA by 27, a vice presidency by 33. Face it, Bobby boy, some people just don't have what it takes."

"Sorry, Dad."

HOPE IN POWERLESSNESS

Much too often the circumstances of our world cause us to feel powerless and vulnerable. Perhaps the value of vulnerability and the hope of powerlessness comes from having to rely upon God.

EL SHADDAI

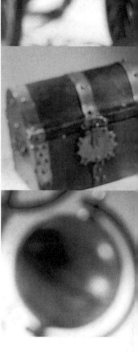

This session will look at the power of God.

GETTING STARTED

Throughout history, humans have struggled against the limitations of language to express the fullness of God's power and majesty. The late singer-songwriter Rich Mullins penned one of the most popular praise songs of the Eighties using one of the most popular words of the day: *awesome.* More than a century and a half before, hymn writer Robert Grant used the vocabulary of his generation to strike a similar chord: *"His chariots of wrath the deep thunderclouds form, and dark is His path on the wings of the storm."* From the psalmists of ancient Israel to the gospel hip-hop artists of the new millennium, God's greatness has been sung by God's people: "The God of glory thunders" (Psalm 29:3); "God is supernatural. Yeah, yeah, yeah" (gospel rap artists, DC Talk).

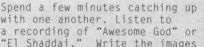
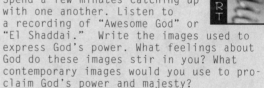

Spend a few minutes catching up with one another. Listen to a recording of "Awesome God" or "El Shaddai." Write the images used to express God's power. What feelings about God do these images stir in you? What contemporary images would you use to proclaim God's power and majesty?

GOD ALMIGHTY

The early patriarchs borrowed the language of their predecessors as well as their neighbors to express their covenant relationship to the God who called Abram to a new life "on the road." *Shaddai*, "the Mountain One," from Mesopotamian roots; and *El*, a common Semitic word used to designate "god" and the name for a Canaanite god. The words were combined to form *El Shaddai*, which is translated "God Almighty" in the Old Testament. This phrase is understood in several ways: God of the mountains, God of the deities, and God with breasts, which is closely associated with fertility and the blessing of life (Genesis 49:25). The priestly tradition in the Bible presents the ancestors as using this name before they learned the sacred name given to Moses during the Exodus. (In Exodus 6:6-8, the word translated "LORD" is YHWH.)

Relationship was truly at the heart of the ancient titles for God: Abram's "shield" (Genesis 15:1), "the Fear of Isaac" (31:42), "the Mighty One of Jacob" (49:24). These titles expressed the patriarchs' understanding of the relational aspects of God's nature. The relationships were very personal, separating the religion of the Hebrew people from those of its contemporary cultures.

ALL IN ALL

Modern theology continues the discourse concerning God's nature by identifying the attributes of God, characteristics that are unique to the Divine. Traditional theology used the

BIBLE

Read aloud Deuteronomy 32:39 and 1 Samuel 2:6-8. Each of the selected Scriptures contains proclamations of God. What do they reveal about God's power? about God's nature? What is your response to these expressions of God's power? How do you think God can be both all powerful and all good?

Power: Using or Abusing Our Potential

word *omnipotence* to describe God as being
all powerful. The limits of human language
and logic create as many conundrums as
they seek to solve. If God is all powerful,
can God do anything, or
can God do only those things that are consistent with God's
nature? This leads to
the question of theodicy,
the attempt to explain
God's goodness when
evil exists in the world
God created. Is God
capable of preventing
suffering and evil in the
world, or is God merely
unwilling to do so? For
many, this dilemma of
discipleship proves
insurmountable.

Rabbi Harold S.
Kushner, a clergyman
and counselor, wrestled
with these questions of faith in his best-
seller, *When Bad
Things Happen to
Good People.*
Kushner's theologi-
cal inquiry was
propelled from the
abstract to the
intensely personal following his young son's
death from a rare, degenerative disorder.

All in All
Debate the age-old theological/
philosophical question, Is God able to
create a stone too heavy for God to lift? How do
you understand *omnipotence*? Do you believe God
is all-powerful? Explain. What do you think about
the idea that there are limits to what God *can* do?
to what God *will* do?

How do you respond when natural disasters are
referred to as "acts of God"? Do you think God
causes earthquakes, floods, or tidal waves? Why or
why not? How do you respond to those who claim
that illness, injury, or untimely death happen
according to God's plan? How do you respond to the
idea that everything that happens in the world—
the good and the bad—is part of God's plan? that
suffering and evil contradict God's will for
humanity? In what ways might tragedies redefine our
responses?

God's Power and Free Will
Would you be willing to trade your free will
to live in a world without suffering or
evil? Why or why not? Read Genesis 2:15-17. Why do you
think God would plant the tree of the knowledge of
good and evil in the middle of Eden?

El Shaddai

While never losing his trust in God's compassion and love, his ultimate conclusion proved somewhat controversial: Kushner forgave God for not being perfect or creating a perfect world. He forgave God's "limitations." Other believers respond differently. The traditional folk hymn "Farther Along" speaks of an unquestioning acceptance that the answers are not to be understood in this life. "We'll understand it all by and by."

GOD'S POWER AND FREE WILL

Some people of faith understand the existence of evil as necessary in order for free will to exist. The "necessary evil" provides a choice between God and the alternative. Others see evil as the by-product of a fallen humanity.

To be honest, most of us would like to see God take control of and fix all the bad things that happen in the world. It's quite a different matter, though, when it comes to God controlling us. We want free will when we decide how to spend our time and money, whom we love, whom we hate, how to live.

WRESTLING WITH FAITH

The struggle between human and divine will is poignantly illustrated in the life of one of salvation history's most fascinating characters, Jacob, the son of Isaac. Heir to the promise of God through his grandfather Abraham, Jacob's life was a series of power struggles, beginning in the womb as he and his twin Esau vied for position. Esau emerged first, securing his birthright as the oldest son;

CASE STUDY

Use the case study "An Omnipotent God, a Suffering World", on pages 75-76 or a personal experience to wrestle with the question of why innocent people suffer. Share your questions and conclusions.

What are some examples in which the suffering of a person or a group has ultimately proved beneficial?

but Jacob was close on his heels. Jacob became his mother's favorite son. Later, he bought his famished brother's birthright for a bowl of lentil soup and, with mom's guidance, tricked their aged, ailing father into bestowing his one-and-only blessing upon his number-two son rather than his favorite first-born son, Esau.

Fearing his brother's wrath, Jacob fled to a new land where new struggles awaited him. In this new land, Jacob was duped—first into marrying the wrong sister and then into years of servitude in his father-in-law's household. When Jacob finally wrangled his way out of Laban's service, he packed up his wives, concubines, children, and flocks and headed for home. Along the way, he learned that Esau was heading toward the entourage. Remembering his brother's old promise to kill him, Jacob sent a gift-laden messenger to Esau.

Jacob sent his family and possessions on ahead, and he remained alone with his thoughts and prayers. During the night an anonymous "man" visited Jacob and wrestled with him until dawn.

The Scripture exemplifies the power of names in the days of the patriarchs. The wrestler asked for Jacob's name then gave him a new one: Israel, "for you have striven with God and with humans, and have prevailed" (Genesis 32:28). Jacob was left with a limp and a new identity. He asked the mysterious visitor's name but instead received a blessing. It was then that Jacob realized that he had been struggling with God. "I have seen God face to face, and yet my life is preserved" (verse 30). Jacob named the place of their encounter Peniel, which means "face of God."

LOOK CLOSER

Wrestling God
Read Genesis 32. Discuss Jacob's wrestling match with God. Why do you think God allowed Jacob to prevail? What does the story reveal to you about God's nature? What does it reveal about God's power?

Have you ever found yourself wrestling with God? What aspects of faith provide the biggest struggle for you?

El Shaddai

BY THE POWER OF THE NAME

The true "name" of God, so elusive to Jacob, would not be revealed until God spoke to Moses several generations later "in a flame of fire out of a bush" (Exodus 3:2). God called Moses by name and commanded him to confront none other than Egypt's pharaoh on God's behalf: "I am the God of your father, the God of Abraham, the God of Isaac, and the God of Jacob" (verse 6). The God of covenant, the God of relationship, was coming down to deliver the Hebrew slaves. God's promise to be with Moses, however, was not enough—Moses wanted a name. "If I come to the Israelites and say to them, 'The God of your ancestors has sent me to you,' and they ask me, 'What is his name?' what shall I say to them? God said to Moses, 'I AM WHO I AM. . . . This is my name forever, / and this my title for all generations' " (verses 13-15).

SMALL GROUP

By the Power of the Name
Read Exodus 3 aloud as a drama with a narrator, God, and Moses. What do you learn about God in this chapter? Why would God use a human to bring about justice instead of speaking directly to the Egyptians? How do you respond when you must resist evil activities? What do you think of God's name, "I am who I am"? What does the divine name reveal about who God is for us? What does it reveal about God's power?

GOD'S POWER IN A WORD

Neither Jacob nor Moses could coerce God into disclosing God's name or nature. It is only through God's willing *self*-revelation that humankind is given a glimpse into the depths of the divine. "I am." God was not created. God has no beginning or end. God simply is. Human beings are not in control of their Creator: "I will be who I will be." And yet, in both stories, God's power is never exerted apart from God's compassion. Jacob is not blessed because of or in spite of his conniving ways. He is

blessed on the basis of Yahweh's promise. In the encounter with Moses, the God of Israel communicated that God saw the suffering of the chosen ones and was moved to act on their behalf.

THE WORD

"In the beginning was the Word, and the Word was with God, and the Word was God" (John 1:1). *Logos* is a Greek concept that suggests reason, thought, and form as well as the spoken word. In Genesis, God "speaks" the creation into existence. The use of the Greek word in John's Gospel suggests that the form, the reasoning power, and the motive for Creation is revealed through Jesus the Christ who was "in the beginning with God." John says further, "All things came into being through him, and without him not one thing came into being" (verse 3). In John's view, God's self is clearly revealed to us in the person of Jesus the Christ, God's Word made flesh. It is the Christ, co-existent with the Creator from the beginning, who incarnates the fullness of God's nature and God's love. God is our power source. We identify God's power in Jesus.

DISCUSS

Your Name
Do you know the meaning of your name? If you can, consult a baby name book to find the root or meaning of the names of members of your group. If there are parents in the group, discuss the process they used for naming their children. Were the names picked for family significance, the sound of the name, or the meaning? Does your name reveal anything about you?

BIBLE

The Word
Working in pairs, read John 1. (Read verses 1-18 closely; skim verses 19-51.) Compare the beginning of the chapter with the beginning of the first chapter of Genesis. What similarities do you find? What do you think John was trying to say about Jesus?

List the power statements made about God's Word, Jesus, in verses 1-18. Which, to you, is the strongest image of Christ's power in this passage? What power is given to those who believe in him?

Read verse 12 aloud. What does it mean to have the power to become a child of God? What power does a child of God possess?

IN A WORD, JESUS

Living as a mortal, Jesus withstood temptation, embraced the dispossessed, healed the hurting, and challenged the status quo. By taking up his cross and laying down his life, Jesus brought about humankind's *atonement*, our literal *at-one-ment* with God. He

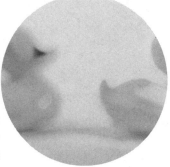

brought the kingdom of God into our midst and opened the kingdom of heaven to those he had redeemed.

By looking to his example, we can learn what true power is. We can, in his image, become conduits for God's power in today's world by allowing God's Spirit to work in and through us. And, like Jesus, we can recharge ourselves at any time by keeping ourselves grounded in God through study, private prayer, and public worship.

SMALL GROUP

Jesus
Form three teams. Read one or more of the following Scriptures.

Luke 7:1-16
Luke 8:22-25
Luke 23:32-43

For each Scripture answer the following: What aspect of Jesus' power is revealed in the encounter? Over what things or people does Jesus have authority? How did those who witnessed the event respond? What aspects of God's nature are revealed in Jesus' actions? What do you learn of God from this encounter?

Which response to Jesus' power seems most like your own? How have you experienced God's power in the world today? How and when has God's power been revealed in your life?

CLOSE

Create a Psalm of Praise
Look back at the contemporary images you used to express your understanding and experience of God's power from the opening of this session. Working together, use these and additional images to create a psalm. A good way to begin might be by completing the following sentences: "Our God is . . ." or "Praise God who . . ."

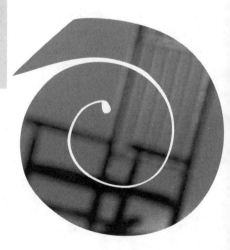

THE DARK SIDE OF THE FORCE

This session will examine images of the "powers of evil" in the Bible and in contemporary life.

GETTING STARTED

The ongoing struggle between the "forces" or "powers" of good and evil is a unifying theme of the *Star Wars* movies. Fans are fascinated with the character of Darth Vader, a powerful Jedi knight who succumbed to the "dark side of the force" to serve the aims of the evil Emperor.

The same struggle between good and evil is the theme of the movie *The Exorcist*. Nearly thirty years after its premiere, *The Exorcist* still tops most polls as the scariest movie of all time. The film's subject matter, a young girl's possession by a particularly nasty demon, is still raising hair—and money— across the world. Upon its initial release, ticket lines and picket lines surrounded theaters. Billy Graham urged the public to stay away, while the Roman Catholic Church upheld the film, providing ordained "technical advisors" as well as occasional blessings

> **START**
>
> Greet one another and welcome any newcomers. Pray the Lord's Prayer together. What does it mean to you to pray "deliver us from evil"? Why would Jesus believe it was necessary to teach the disciples to "pray then in this way"? (Matthew 6:9).

for the set, cast, and crew. William Friedkin, the film's director, is still being asked about its impact after all these years, especially in light of its recent re-release and DVD debut. Friedkin, who considers himself "a religious person and a believer in God," feels there is more to *The Exorcist* than a good scare. "I would like to think that it is also giving people the opportunity to contemplate spiritual matters."

SPIRITUAL MATTERS

Theologian Walter Wink would probably agree with Friedkin's assessment. Wink believes that angels, demons, and the devil have become the "unmentionables of our culture" because our modern, materialistic world has "no categories, no vocabulary, [and] no presuppositions" for understanding the experiences of those whose encounters with these such beings are recorded in the Bible. A 2001 Barna Research Group poll on US religious beliefs supports his assertions. Among Roman Catholics, only 17 percent of those surveyed believe that Satan is real. While the percentage is somewhat higher in nondenominational faith communities, only 20 percent of the mainline Protestants polled affirm the same belief.

In a three-part series, *The Powers*, Wink explores the biblical and cultural roots of these invisible forces, as well as their "incarnations" in the present age. In the second book of his trilogy, *Unmasking The Powers*, he pays special attention to the debate among people of faith concerning Satan. Is *Satan* a title that describes the activity of a member of God's own council, or is it the proper name of one particular being of preeminent power, the "evil one"—the ultimate monster under the bed? For Wink, the question is not the *if* of Satan's existence, but the *how*? How do we experience Satan in today's world?

Tell Jokes
Think of any jokes that feature the devil. Take several minutes to share a few of these stories. What, if anything, do they reveal about our cultural understanding of evil? What is your understanding of evil now?

THE DEVIL MADE ME DO IT

Like *The Exorcist*, another hit of the 1970's has found a new audience by way of DVD and the retro network TVLand. *The Flip Wilson Show*, one of the highest-rated programs of its day, ushered a new catch phrase into the American vernacular: "The devil made me do it." Geraldine, the wisecracking wild woman played by Flip

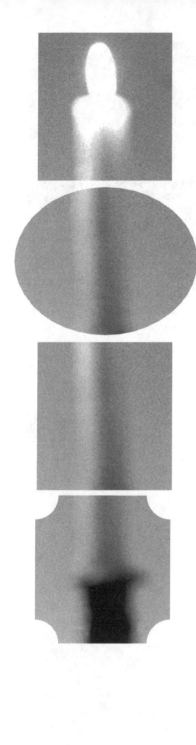

Wilson, delivered this punch line at least once in every episode to explain away her multitude of sins.

The joke, however, exemplifies an ancient "cosmology," a picture of the universe with heaven above, the earth in the middle, and an underworld beneath the earth. Human beings, to a great extent, may be understood in this worldview as pawns on a cosmic chessboard in the ongoing contest between good and evil. While this cosmological understanding has faded from prominence, it still informs the core of theological understanding for many people of faith—God struggling against Satan to "win" human souls. Before returning to the *how* of our experience of Satan, it is helpful to look first at the biblical roots of our understanding of Satan.

Job

If the Book of Job comes to mind as a contest between God and Satan, look again. Satan is testing Job's faithfulness on God's behalf. He is not so much struggling to gain Job's allegiance to his own evil purposes as he is determining if Job's devotion is dependent on his prosperity. In this heavenly courtroom where God sits on the bench, Satan may best be understood as a prosecuting attorney. Satan has no power apart from God.

Peter

"Simon, Simon, listen! Satan has demanded to sift all of you like wheat" (Luke 22:31). Satan was again serving a divine purpose: separating true faithfulness from false reliance on our own righteousness. While Jesus prayed for his disciples, Peter fell asleep. Relying on his own abilities, Peter, when tested by Satan, was found lacking.

Jesus

If we think of Satan as the tester, Jesus' temptation in the wilderness was not a case of God abandoning him to the evil one, but making sure that Jesus was aware of his choices. In Matthew and Luke, when Satan tempted Jesus to jump from the pinnacle of the Temple, Satan used Scripture (Psalm 91:11-12) to test Jesus' will. (Temptation never looks particularly "evil," does it?) The devil's taunts were consistent with who Jesus really was: He had power to produce bread in abundance; he had power to call upon angels; he will have power to rule the kingdoms of the world. However, Jesus chose God's will, God's timing.

The devil couldn't make Jesus do anything he wasn't willing to do. Walter Wink contends that Satan is the "god of this world" (2 Corinthians 4:4) only because we have made him so by consciously choosing to abandon God's will in favor of our own aims. The voice of the slanderer tells us exactly what we want to hear or entreats us to hopelessness and despair—always at the opportune time. We empower Satan every time we turn from God's truth to the "father of lies" (John 8:44).

In Matthew 12:22-32, some of the Pharisees sought to discredit Jesus by claiming that his power to cast out demons came from Beelzebul—the devil. Jesus implied that the accusation was the unforgivable sin of blasphemy against the Spirit (verses 31-32). By accusing Jesus of using the power of Beelzebul, they are, in effect, defining God's will and God's work as evil.

The Devil Made Me Do It
Working in groups of two or three, read one or more of the following passages:
Job 1:6-12
Luke 4:1-13
Matthew 16:21-23
Luke 22:1-6, 31-34

Based on all you've discussed to this point, as well as the information in "Bible 101," how do you understand Satan in each account? How do you understand the power of Satan in each passage? the power of free will or human choice? God's will? What does the sentence "The devil made me do it!" say to you about personal responsibility? about blaming? about the power of evil?

EVIL

There are biblical accounts of demonic possession, as well as faith traditions that accept and document such occurrences in the present day. Other people of faith interpret these experiences as psychiatric or seizure disorders that were not recognized in biblical times. Some view these stories as descriptions of "personal demons," such as addictions, guilt, and unresolved issues, for example, that impede our psychosocial functioning in the world.

BIBLE

Read Matthew 12:22-32. How do you understand Jesus' response to the accusation that the power to cast out demons came from Beelzebul?

Whether we understand evil as an autonomous, external power—with or without a name—or an internal wrestling of will, most of us can say we've experienced what *The Merriam-Webster Dictionary* defines as "something that brings sorrow, distress, or calamity." Evil is real.

The Holocaust exemplifies one of the greatest evils of human history. The Third Reich targeted Jews, gypsies, homosexuals, and others for extermination. Many historians believe Adolf Hitler, who motivated and mobilized Germany to pursue these policies, suffered from mental illness. Many people of faith explain his actions as being the work of Satan. But were all those who imposed Hitler's will mentally ill? Did Satan take possession of everyone who did Hitler's bidding? Or was evil empowered by the failure of human will to stand up to a small group of human beings and say no in the

SMALL GROUP

Evil
Form groups of three and discuss the following questions: What are the greatest examples of evil you can think of from   history? What factors cause you to define an event or action as evil? How would you define evil?

Select one of your examples to examine more fully. How was this evil manifest? What situations in the world made it possible for such a thing to happen? Do you attribute this occurrence to demonic forces, to Satan, or to human will?

What, if anything, could have prevented something like this from happening? What responsibility, if any, do Christians have for addressing or challenging evil?

name of Jesus Christ? People of faith struggle with such questions as they seek explanations for the horrifying realities of evil.

ABSOLUTE POWER

John Emerich Edward Dalberg Acton, 19th century historian (who, as a Roman Catholic, was prohibited from entering Cambridge University), observed that "power tends to corrupt, and absolute power corrupts absolutely." Sadly, Lord Acton's proverb has proven itself throughout human history but only when that power comes from human sources.

"His divine power has given us everything needed for life and godliness, through the knowledge of him who called us by his own glory and goodness. Thus he has given us, through these things, his precious and very great promises, so that through them you may escape from the corruption that is in the world because of lust, and may become participants of the divine nature" (2 Peter 1:3-4).

Lust is not necessarily a sexual reference but describes those things that tempt us away from God. God's power cannot be corrupted by human desire. That's why keeping ourselves grounded in God's will is the only absolute way to keep our connection to the Source of true power. God gives us freedom of will and choice, and at the same time, God reaches out to us and empowers us to live God's way.

SCARY STUFF

David Bruce, film reviewer and creator of *hollywoodjesus.com*, a

Absolute Power
What is your response to the phrase "power tends to corrupt, and absolute power corrupts absolutely." What examples come to mind? Who, in your view, has been corrupted by power? What was the source of his/her/their power?

Can you think of any powerful men or women who have, in your opinion, remained "good"? How do they avoid corruption? What is the source of their power?

Scary Stuff
What is your response to each of the following statements?

Unseen powers really exist.
We can't control everything.
We have to submit to God—to pray "thy will be done" (or even "lead us not into temptation") as fervently as we pray "deliver us from evil."

Do you think submitting to God's will is scary? Why or why not?

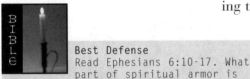

Best Defense
Read Ephesians 6:10-17. What part of spiritual armor is defensive? What part is offensive? Do you find any irony in battle images being used to proclaim a "gospel of peace"? Where do we go for our spiritual equipment? Describe what basic training might look like for those preparing to do battle against evil.

Stand in a circle and hold hands. Do you feel more powerful when you are standing together or standing alone? Those who are willing may offer spoken prayers that the Spirit may empower you to uphold one another in your journeys of faith. Others may pray silently. Pray that your discipleship may withstand the temptation to seek the world's power over God's.

Web site devoted to "pop culture from a spiritual point of view," believes the most frightening aspects of *The Exorcist* are the spiritual questions and truths it raises. Acknowledging that life cannot always be controlled is part of what Bruce calls the "real horror" of the film and, with that, the possibility that these demonic forces really do exist. The scariest thing for believers, however, just might be accepting the idea "that we may have to submit to God."

We can't control life. Evil exists. Temptation is real. But God doesn't leave us defenseless. Paul says it well in Romans 8:38-39: "For I am convinced that neither death, nor life, nor angels, nor rulers, nor things present, nor things to come, nor powers, nor height, nor depth, nor anything else in all creation, will be able to separate us from the love of God in Christ Jesus our Lord."

THE BEST DEFENSE

The Jedi knights used light sabers to battle those who, like Darth Vader and the evil Emperor, had fallen to the "dark side." Christians are equipped a bit differently for our battle against the slanderer. We are given the "whole armor" of God, so that we may be able to withstand "on that evil day" (Ephesians 6:13). It may not be as flashy as the Hollywood version, but it's a lot more effective. The promise of Christian faith is that good will ultimately win and that God gives us the power to choose God's way.

DUI: DISCIPLES UNDER THE INFLUENCE

This session will explore what it means to be empowered by the Holy Spirit.

SETTING STARTED

Picture it. A sound like a mighty wind. Tongues of fire. It may not be the first picture of church that comes to mind, but it is a picture of the church as it first appeared on the day of Pentecost. When the Holy Spirit came upon the disciples with power from above, the church was born—complete with special effects.

Just fifty days before, the disciples had gone into hiding for fear of ending up like Jesus. After the dramatic and empowering appearance of the Holy Spirit, these same disciples proclaimed their Lord's crucifixion and resurrection boldly to all who would listen and spoke in languages they did not know. They spoke of God's "deeds of power" without as much as a second thought to saving their own skins. And what an evangelism program! "So those who welcomed his message were baptized, and that day about three thousand persons were added" (Acts 2:41).

START

Greet one another. Welcome any newcomers. Discuss how your church celebrates Pentecost Sunday. What does the word *pentecostal* suggest to you? Is it a positive or negative image? Why? Has anyone in your class attended a service at a pentecostal church? In what sense are all churches pentecostal?

BREATHE ON ME, BREATH OF GOD

While Pentecost is the event marking the Holy Spirit's outpouring on the entire community following Jesus' resurrection and ascension, the Spirit of God, God's presence and power, has been at work since the beginning. *Ruah* or *ruach*, the Hebrew word for *spirit*, can also mean "wind" or "breath." The "Spirit of the Lord" is a life-breathing force, the "wind from God [that] swept over the face of the waters" at Creation (Genesis 1:2). God's Spirit is creative, instructive, redemptive, proactive power that equipped the patriarchs, prophets, and kings of Israel for living out the covenant. In Old Testament understanding, the Spirit of God is a life-giving force that inspires and empowers. The first description of the Spirit as holy appears in Psalm 51:11; only in one other instance (Isaiah 63:10-11) does "holy spirit" appear in the Old Testament.

THE SPIRIT OF THE LORD

The Spirit of the Lord rested upon Moses and later extended to the seventy elders of Israel (Numbers 11:16-17). The Spirit of the Lord brought Ezekiel to the valley of dry bones and breathed new life into the skeletons of post-exilic Israel in an act of divine resuscitation (Ezekiel 37). And the Spirit of the Lord carried Elijah, in the words of Obadiah, "I know not where" (1 Kings 18:12), as God had need of him in an act of divine relocation. God's Spirit moved in and among God's chosen ones in the unfolding story of salvation.

THE HOLY SPIRIT

In the New Testament, the Holy Spirit is manifest in more personal terms that form the basis of later Trinitarian doctrine. In 381 A.D., the Council of Constantinople affirmed the Holy Spirit's divinity as coequal with that of God the Father and God the Son. The Holy Spirit's power overshadowed Mary and brought about the birth of Jesus (Luke 1:26-35). The Holy Spirit compelled the newly baptized Jesus to enter the wilderness where he would face temptation by the devil (Matthew 4; Mark 1; Luke 4). And the Holy Spirit invigorated and empowered the early church to proclaim its risen Savior in the face of persecution if not certain death. The Holy Spirit came upon and filled Christ's disciples for service in his kingdom, imparting a variety of gifts to fulfill a variety of tasks.

Read Joel 2:28-32, the prophecy quoted by Peter on the day of Pentecost (Acts 2:17-21). Take note of those persons upon whom God's Spirit will be poured. What human distinctions are rendered meaningless in "the day of the Lord"? Who is exempt from the outpouring of the Spirit? What might this mean for the church today?

Distribute hymnals or songbooks and search the index for songs about the Holy Spirit and/or Pentecost. What images of power do you find in these songs? Which, if any, speak to your experience of God? Choose a song, and sing it.

"I WILL NOT LEAVE YOU ORPHANED"

In John's Gospel, Jesus promised that, in his absence, the "Spirit of truth," the "Advocate," would remain with the disciples forever (John 14:15-26). The word in the Greek text is *parakletos*, which means "comforter," "advocate," "intercessor," or "consoler." The Advocate is given to the church through Jesus Christ and is the immanent presence of God in believers and in the community of faith. As such, the Holy Spirit may also be understood as the Spirit of Christ that dwells in and among those who bear his name.

Look up "Spirit of the Lord" and "Holy Spirit" in a concordance. Pick several of the passages at random from the Old and New Testaments. What does the Spirit do in each passage? How do you understand the Holy Spirit?

The empty tomb and Mary's proclamation, "I have seen the Lord," were not enough to pry the disciples from the safety of their hiding place on Easter evening (John 20:19). Not until Jesus appeared in their midst and breathed the Spirit into them did they take the first step into their new lives as missionaries of a new reality. Once again, the divine breath of life came sweeping through Christ's people.

PETER: BEFORE AND AFTER

Just as power is best understood in concrete situations and applications, the Spirit is perhaps best understood as it is embodied in the lives of the faithful. One of the clearest examples of the transforming power of God's Spirit can be seen in the life of Peter. Two millennia before "The Rock" of *WrestleMania*, the Rock upon which Jesus would build his church dropped his fishing net to follow the Messiah. (The name *Peter* means "rock.") The rough and tumble everyman promised to stay with Jesus to the end. However, when the going got rough, the rough one got going—straight into hiding with the rest of the disciples.

The potential Jesus had seen in this ordinary man would come to fruition in the Spirit's own time. The same Peter who fled in the night would go on to claim his power in the name of his Lord. Filled by the Holy Spirit, Peter would preach, heal, and make disciples with a boldness that others could not comprehend. While there is no direct biblical witness, tradition teaches that Peter would eventually follow Jesus to the end, bearing his own literal cross. He counted himself unworthy to die in the same manner as his Savior and asked to be crucified upside down.

DISCIPLESHIP: BEFORE AND AFTER

The call to Spirit-led discipleship is not necessarily a call to martyrdom. The Spirit will call and empower the disciples of Jesus Christ to continue his mission in the world. What we cannot achieve on our own comes in the form of a gift from the very same Spirit. Through the Spirit, everyday, ordinary, human Christians will be able to work miracles, to heal, to prophesy. "All these are activated by one and the same Spirit, who allots to each one individually just as the Spirit chooses" (1 Corinthians 12:11).

With the power comes the authority to act in the name of Jesus Christ. In his second letter to the church in Corinth, Paul speaks of the church as a "new creation" in Christ: "Everything old has passed away; see, everything has become new!" (2 Corinthians 5:17). More than a transformed creation, we are ambassadors for Christ, those given not only the right but the responsibility to act with the full authority of the One who sends us into the world. God's ministry of reconciliation has been entrusted to us. Those who have been transformed in Christ are called to become transformers in his name.

Form teams of two or three. Discuss: What do the changes in Peter's life suggest to us about our own relationship with God?

What changes might we as individuals or as congregations expect to experience by allowing the Holy Spirit to work through us?

Discipleship: Before and After
Choose a partner. Read the following Scriptures:

Matthew 10:1-8
Luke 9:1-6
John 20:22-23

What power and authority are given to the disciples of Jesus Christ through the Holy Spirit? Do you feel empowered to do these things in the name of Christ? Why or why not? In what ways do you think the Spirit has empowered you?

DUI

The question has often been asked, "If practicing Christianity were against the law, could they find enough evidence in your life to convict you?" On the day of Pentecost, the believers were so caught up in the Spirit's power that the more skeptical onlookers were certain they must be drunk. However, a Breathalyzer would have revealed

DUI
Read Acts 2:38-47. How does the Scripture describe life empowered by the Holy Spirit? Based on this passage and your discussion of this passage, how would you characterize a Spirit-led life in the contemporary world?

something quite different: the Breath of
God, the rushing wind of the Spirit giving
new life to the body of Christ—the newborn
church.

That's not to say that God's Spirit can
only be manifest in dramatic, ecstatic
expressions like those of Pentecost. The
Spirit, like the wind, "blows where it chooses"
(John 3:8). God's Spirit is as powerfully
present in the silence of a Quaker meeting
house as it is in a hand-clapping, music-
filled, exuberant service of praise. The
influence of the Spirit is measured best
not by the style—or volume—of worship, but in the servanthood that begins
when the church service ends. The true
evidence of a Christian life—a Spirit-
led, transformed life—can only be
assessed outside the sanctuary doors in
the 24/7 of what our families, coworkers, acquaintances, and friends witness in our words and actions. "Church"
is more than the building or what happens in the building. Church is also the
people of God, called, equipped, empowered, and turned loose in the world.

Pick one of the Holy
Spirit songs you identi-
fied earlier in this ses-
sion to sing together in closing.
Close your eyes and spend a few
moments focusing on your breathing.
As you feel your breath moving in
and out, pray for God's Spirit to
be breathed into your life. Imagine
your incoming breath as the Holy
Spirit's power and love entering
you and your outgoing breath as the
Holy Spirit's power and love moving
through you and out into the world.
Listen quietly to any insight you
gain about how you might serve God
by serving others. Celebrate the
life-giving power of God in Jesus
Christ.

THE CHURCH POWERFUL, THE CHURCH EMPOWERED

This session will examine how the church is empowered by God and how the church has used or abused its power in the world.

GETTING STARTED

"All who believed were together and had all things in common; they would sell their possessions and goods and distribute the proceeds to all, as any had need. Day by day, as they spent much time together in the temple, they broke bread at home and ate their food with glad and generous hearts, praising God and having the goodwill of all the people" (Acts 2:44-47a). Following Pentecost, the church was off and running: sharing, praising, giving thanks, meeting people's needs. All too soon, however, the old temptations, divisions, and power struggles would find their way into the body.

Even those of us who love the church, who are the church, have to admit that our witness in the world has often been diminished by our internal squabbles, fearfulness, and hypocrisies. In the words of one theologian, "the church is

Getting Started
Catch up with one another. Welcome newcomers. Tell about your earliest memories of church. What did you like most about your experience? What did you like least? In your understanding, what does church mean?

like Noah's ark; if it weren't for the storm raging on the outside, we wouldn't be able to stand the stench on the inside."

INSIDE

Some of the earliest attacks against the church actually originated *inside* the body. As new believers were moved by the Spirit to sell their possessions and live in mutual sharing, a plan very similar to the one Moses had delivered to the newly freed Hebrew slaves, some had trouble getting with the program. Ananias and his wife Sapphira sold a piece of their property but conspired to keep a portion of the proceeds. Confronted with his lie, Ananias dropped dead at Peter's feet. When Sapphira arrived, as yet unaware of her husband's fate, she too withheld the actual purchase price. Her subsequent demise was as immediate as her mate's.

Complaints by the Hellenists (Greek Christians) about the Hebrews' (Jewish Christians) neglect of their widows began to surface. Questions about Gentile converts created controversy. Must new believers become Jews (*circumcised* Jews) in order to become Christians? Could food considered unclean under the law of Moses suddenly become acceptable in light of the new covenant? Decisions, decisions. Practical issues in the everyday life of believers prompted decisions. Perhaps the most important one was a question: Just who is really in charge?

Paul's letters were intended to be read when the body gathered for worship. Philippians 4:2-9 addresses a confict or disagreement between Euodia and Syntyche. Paul did not elaborate on the disagreement. The Scripture suggests that its resolution was more important to him than who was right. He offered a list of suggestions that have value for the church in all times and in all places. Help one another. Rejoice in the Lord. Be gentle. Don't worry. Give God your requests. Think about things that are true, honorable, just, pure, pleasing, commendable, excellent, and worthy of praise. Paul said that peace will result from such thoughts and actions.

> **BIBLE**
> Read Acts 4:32-5:11. What challenges make you want to know more about the Scripture? Where do you think the apostles' "great power" (Acts 4:33) originated? Why do you think Ananias and Sapphira decided to withhold part of their profit? What connections do you make between their choice and the use or abuse of power? How do you explain their deaths? What does the story say to you about power?

> **DISCUSS**
> **Agree or Disagree**
> Designate one side of the learning area "agree" and the other side "disagree." Decide if you agree or disagree with the following statement, and stand in the area that matches your response. "The church should never have disagreements among its members."

OUTSIDE

External pressures were also exerted against the church. Persecutions threatened to exterminate the church for nearly three centuries. Prior to his own conversion, Paul the

> **BIBLE**
> **Conflict Resolution**
> Read Philippians 4:2-9. What insights can we gain from this passage for approaching conflict and controversy? What do you think would happen if your pastor addressed conflict directly from the pulpit and named those involved?

apostle (a.k.a. Saul of Tarsus) had lived as an enemy of the gospel, approving even the stoning of Stephen. "But Saul was ravaging the church by entering house after house; dragging off both men and women, he committed them to prison" (Acts 8:3). The last imperial persecution of Christians occurred under Diocletian (A.D.284–A.D. 305). Previous persecutions were more local in nature. Persecutions offered such horrors as imprisonment, torture, and execution by wild beasts, beheading, flaying, fire, and the like for those who refused to recant their faith in Christ.

UPSIDE DOWN

Constantine dreamed about a cross in the sky with the words "in this sign conquer" and interpreted his victory in battle as a proof of Christ's power. He was converted to Christianity in 312 A.D.; and upon his conversion, the status quo for the church was turned on its ear. The outlaw faith became the state religion. State religion had little tolerance for free will. The persecuted church became the persecuting church.

The rest, as they say, is history: the Crusades and Inquisitions, witch hunts in Europe and the colonies, slave trading, and the eradication of indigenous peoples by those who invaded and conquered in the name of cross and crown. A church with this kind of power can forget its reliance on God. For years the church sold "indulgences," "holy," get-out-of-jail-free cards for the forgiveness of sins.

Our more recent past is no less tainted by corruption. Some abuses of power are blatant: high-priced TV evangelists preaching piety while practicing promiscuity, sexual abuse by clergy, and cover-ups.

Other abuses are revealed in quieter ways—often in the church's tacit acceptance of a status quo that preys upon the poor and oppressed. And when the world can hear the church, how many times does it only hear Christians yelling at one another? Diversity too often becomes dissension as Christians argue over doctrine and politics. Unity in Christ is denied by intolerance toward those Christians whose theology, worship, social status, accent, and skin color are different from our own. Christians forget that they are all in the same boat.

Read Ephesians 4:15-16. What happens in a church when Christ is not in control? What happens when God's will takes second place to what certain individuals or groups decide? In what ways can a church discern the will of God in the life and mission of the church?

Confessing
Form groups of two or three. Spend a moment or two in silence thinking about some of the wrongs done to you by others. Tell about these only if you are comfortable doing so. Did those who caused you pain ever confess to you? Did they ask for forgiveness? Was that (or should it have been) helpful in your healing? What sins do you think the church needs to confess? Do you think it is easier or more difficult to confess the sins of our ancestors than it is to confess our own sin? the sins of the contemporary church? Explain your response. What connections can you make between power and confession?

NOW YOU ARE THE BODY OF CHRIST

What is it, then, that keeps us from jumping overboard? It all goes back to remembering who we are in relationship to

Onboard
We've spent much of this session discussing what's "wrong" with the church. Develop a list of things that are "right" with the church. What is it that keeps us onboard? Why haven't you given up on organized religion? What might you say to those who have?

God. We are members of the same body—Christ's body—diverse in gifts and appearance but called and equipped for a common purpose: "But speaking the truth in love, we must grow up in every way into him who is the head, into Christ, from whom the whole body, joined and knit together by every ligament with which it is equipped, as each part is working properly, promotes the body's growth in building itself up in love" (Ephesians 4:15-16). When Christ is fully in control, we will stay on course.

A CONFESSING CHURCH

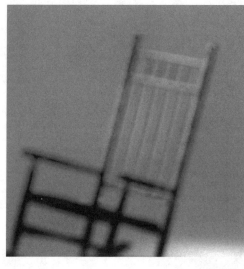

Speaking the truth—even in love—is not always easy. Confronting our sins as the church is no less painful than confronting our sins as individual Christians. The Confessing Church was organized in Germany in 1933 to oppose the Nazis' insistence that the church conform to its racial policies. Though many Christians who assisted those the Nazis persecuted were imprisoned or killed, many in the church did conform: some through their silence, others by claiming the persecution to be the will of God. The Confessing Church named the sin. In the words of deaconess Marga Meusel, "Since when has the evildoer the right to portray his evil deeds as the will of God?" Christ, and not the Third Reich, controlled The Confessing Church.

Other churches have been bold in confessing Christ by confession of their corporate sinfulness. In June 1995, the Southern

Baptist Convention publicly apologized for condoning slavery and racism in its history as a denomination. That same year, the fiftieth anniversary of the end of WWII, the bishops of Japan issued a "resolution for peace," which acknowledged "how inhuman and out of harmony with the gospel were the elements of that war," as well as the church's failure to witness to the will of God.

BACK ONBOARD

Remember the Noah's ark analogy quoted at the beginning of the session? Tempting as it may be sometimes to jump ship, those of us who are Christ's body may instead have to pick up a pitchfork and pitch in. As the church, it's up to us to "clean up our act." If we acknowledge what's wrong with the church and work to embody authentic discipleship, we might help others to see what's right—to see Christ at work in us. Then, we will offer a real alternative to the storm—a gathering of disciples who share, praise, give thanks, and dedicate ourselves to serving Christ by serving Christ's people.

It does involve a certain amount of risk. In the words of author and educator John A. Shedd, "A ship in harbor is safe, but that is not what ships are built for." As called out ones, we can't rest in the harbor forever; in fact, the harbor can be a dangerous place during a storm. Ships can be dashed to pieces in high winds. Under the Spirit's power, the Spirit's breath, we have to get sailing.

CASE STUDIES

Marcus

"My parents are on me to come back to the family church, but I just can't. It's always the same bickering about the same things.

The Church Powerful, the Church Empowered

Some people haven't spoken to each other in years because of a fight over the color of the carpet! I want to go to a church that does something in the world. There's a church close by that operates a soup kitchen and a food bank. They fought to change the zoning laws so a homeless shelter could open in an old warehouse. To me, that's a real church; but my dad thinks a church should be about Jesus—not politics."

Alicia

"Jamal is the sweetest man I've met in ages; he might even be 'the one,' but I wish he could share my faith. He didn't grow up in the church, and he says he's not about to start now. He thinks the church is full of closed-minded hypocrites who want to get in your business and tell you how to live your life. He refuses to attend even one service with me, and lately he's started making plans for us on Sundays. I don't know what to do."

Elizabeth

"Church is not for me! I attended worship on campus a couple of times with my roommate, but I was really turned off. They treated me differently because I didn't speak in tongues. I just didn't feel like I belonged. I have never felt so much like an outsider before, and I never want to feel that way again."

Case Study
Read the accounts of Marcus, Alicia, and Elizabeth. How might you respond in each situation? What would you like each character to do? How do you think Marcus should respond to his father? What should Alicia do in terms of her relationship with Jamal? Has anyone ever told you, like Elizabeth, that you just didn't measure up in terms of your faith? How did you respond? Would you encourage Elizabeth to give the church a second chance? What might you say to her? What do these case studies say to you about the use or abuse of power in the church?

Closing
Paul concluded his discussion of gifts and the body by showing a "more excellent way." Read 1 Corinthians 13 together. What's love got to do with it? What connections do you see between love and power? How might the power of love work to affirm our unity and our diversity? Pray for the church to live in love.

GIVING IT UP TO GOD

This session will look at what it means to give God power over our lives.

GETTING STARTED

Submit, succumb, surrender. Throw in the towel; wave the white flag; yell uncle. Yield. Resign. Acquiesce. Capitulate. Give it up. Do these words and phrases conjure up images of "going with the flow" or images of "going under"? What about when we use them to talk about our faith? Does the idea of *willingly* and *willfully* placing ourselves under the power of the Holy Spirit seem like a "win/lose" proposition? Does surrendering to God feel more like an admission of personal defeat or a proclamation and reclamation of our personal power as people formed and transformed in our Creator's image?

Getting Started
Greet one another. Introduce yourselves to any first-timers. Pray the Lord's Prayer. Focus on the line "thy/your will be done." What are we really asking for in this petition? What needs to happen in order for God's will to prevail on earth? What do you think it means for an individual believer or for a church to pray these words?

NOT MY WILL, BUT . . .

"And going a little farther, he threw himself on the ground and prayed that, if it were possible, the hour might pass from him. He said, 'Abba, Father, for you all things are possible; remove this cup from me; yet, not what I want, but what you want'" (Mark 14:35-36). As Jesus faced his arrest and crucifixion, he prayed that there might be another way, and yet he found in the fullness of his humanity the courage to surrender his will to God. His love for God and for God's people was greater than his fear for his own life.

Jesus prayed for God to intervene, yet Jesus did not resign himself to fate. Jesus chose to commit or submit his actions to God's power. The words *commit* and *submit* are very similar. *Mittere* is the Latin word that means "to cause to go." The Latin root *sub* means "under," and *com* means "with." These words more accurately describe the choice Jesus made in his prayer. Jesus made an agonizing choice to place his own will under and with the power and the will of God,

BIBLE

Not My Will, But . . .
Read Mark 14:35-36. How do you understand God's power in this circumstance of Jesus' life? Jesus' power? What does the Scripture say to you about God? about Jesus' relationship to God? about our relationship to God? How might the ability to say to God "not what I want, but what you want" empower you?

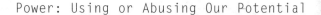

even though he knew the choice would involve suffering and death. "In his anguish he prayed more earnestly, and his sweat became like great drops of blood falling down on the ground" (Luke 22:44).

I SURRENDER...ALL?

Jesus calls those who wish to become his disciples to "take up their cross and follow me" (Matthew 16:24). James, a leader of the church in Jerusalem, thought by many to be Jesus' brother, requires Christians to "submit yourselves therefore to God" (James 4:7). In essence, every time we pray the Lord's Prayer we are asking for God's will to supersede our own; yet *submit* sounds so much like *giving up*—choosing powerlessness. Is that really what we want? Is *that* what God is really asking of us?

I Surrender All?
Do you think anyone can be a disciple, a true follower of Christ, without "submitting" to God? Why or why not? What parts of your life are you comfortable surrendering of God's will? Over what aspects of your life do you want to maintain control? How do you think submitting to God can help you discover God's transforming power of love?

How can we, as Christians, respond to those who use the Bible to put, or keep, others down? What can we say to those who have been subjected to abuse by others who claim biblical authority to do so?

The biblical mandate to submit to God has been abused by those who wish to dominate others. They enforced it as a means of securing their own power. The Bible has been used to condone and uphold such atrocities as slavery, anti-Semitism, corrupt political systems, and violence against women. Images of "lord" and "master," as well as the call to become "slaves" can also be problematic for those whose ancestors were enslaved by a predominantly Christian people who used God's Word to absolve themselves and their actions. American history gives sad testimony to this truth.

To take up one's cross and follow Jesus is to choose the way of love in spite of burdens or limitations. To submit oneself to God is to choose the transforming power of God's love in Christ. Again, these choices are anything but resignation. They are, in fact, empowering.

SO GREAT A CLOUD OF WITNESSES

Great Cloud of Witnesses
Form two groups. Have the first group read Daniel 3:13-30. Have the second group read Acts 7:51-60. Why do you think Shadrach, Meshach, Abednego, and later, Stephen, stood up against such powerful opponents? How do you think they were empowered to remain faithful at such personal risk? What do the stories say to you about human faithfulness? about God's faithfulness? about power?

The Bible gives testimony to those who overcome tyranny through the power of the Holy Spirit. The Book of Daniel is set during the oppressive reign of King Nebuchadnezzar of Babylon, though many scholars accept that it was written during the later persecution of the Jews under Antiochus IV. The stories of Daniel in the lion's den and Shadrach, Meshach, and Abednego in the furnace are often told to children because of their larger-than-life imagery; but they are testimonies to faithfulness and the power of human will. Shadrach, Meshach, and Abednego did not know that God would save them; they only knew that they would remain faithful to God no matter what the cost (Daniel 3:17-18).

Stephen, the first Christian martyr, was not able to subdue his attackers but, "filled with the Holy Spirit," he found the power to gaze into heaven and to call upon God to forgive those who were stoning him (Acts 7:54-60).

Read Hebrews 11:1-12:2. How can reflecting upon the lives of these biblical "heroes" of our faith in the company of other Christians help us to live bolder, more "powerful" lives?

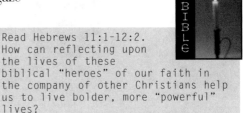

Hebrews 11:1–12:2 is an account of a great cloud of witnesses. The writer of this epistle was giving encouragement to first-century believers who were trying to remain hopeful as they waited for Christ's return. They are reminded of the faith of those who went forward on God's promise without living to see the coming of God's Messiah.

Post-biblical history is full of other examples of those whose lives were empowered by the Holy Spirit. They, too, have taken stands in the name of their God, often transforming society in the process.

Rosa Parks

In 1955, Rosa Parks refused to give up her bus seat to a white man. In 1999, she was awarded the Congressional Gold Medal for the quiet defiance that spurred a social revolution in America. Credited as a catalyst of the civil rights movement for African Americans, Rosa Parks gives the credit for her courage to God. Looking back on that day she writes, "Since I have always been a strong believer in God, I knew that He was with me, and only He could get me through that next step."

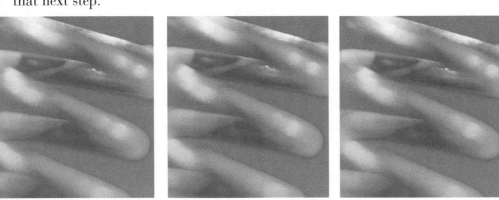

Giving It Up to God

Read the accounts of Rosa Parks, Millard Fuller, and Oscar Romero, sharing any additional information you may know about them. Do these three strike you as powerful people? Why? What has each been able to accomplish through trust in and submission to God's will? What is (or will be) their legacy? What was the cost of their actions?

Try to put yourself in the place of each. At the "moment of truth" faced by Parks, Fuller, and Romero, do you think you would have been able to take the same action? What things might have stopped you? How does the faith of these witnesses encourage you to make your own decision of faith and surrender?

Millard Fuller

Even though Millard Fuller was a millionaire by the age of 29, he and his wife, Linda, struggled in their marriage as they gained in fortune. Together, they decided to trade in the American Dream for a second chance at a Christ-centered marriage, selling everything and giving their money to the poor. Over half a million men, women, and children now have a roof over their heads thanks to the Fullers, founders of Habitat for Humanity International. In Fuller's understanding, "I see life as both a gift and a responsibility. My responsibility is to use what God has given me to help His people in need."

Oscar Romero

Archbishop Oscar Romero was a likely candidate for going along to get along. Elected by conservative bishops, Romero was not expected to make waves in politically turbulent El Salvador (Spanish for "the Savior"). For years he had remained silent in the face of the oppression and violence that plagued the poor of his native land. And then a fellow priest, Rutilio Grande, was murdered along with two of his parishioners—an elderly man and a child—while standing up for the rights of farm workers. The timid Romero was transformed into an impassioned advocate for the Salvadoran peasants. In a speech given on March 23, 1980, he said, "Any human order to kill must be subordinate to the law of God, which says, 'Thou shalt not kill.' It is high time you obeyed your consciences rather than sinful orders. The church cannot remain silent before such an abomination." One day later, Oscar Romero was shot and killed as he celebrated Mass.

TAKING THE PLUNGE

Submitting to God is so much more than passive acceptance of the capricious or arbitrary will of a divine being. Nineteenth-century philosopher Soren Kierkegaard maintained that coming to Christ requires taking a "leap of faith," one that can only be undertaken with "fear and trembling" because of the "absolute uncertainty that underlies it." In contemporary terms, we might compare it to skydiving or to a bungee cord leap. A leap of faith suggests an active, perhaps terror-filled, choice. Yet, the leap of faith leads to a transformed life. Christianity is a Resurrection faith, which means that no matter what dangers exist in the leap, the life and love of Christ will sustain the one who "takes the plunge."

LOOK CLOSER

Taking the Plunge
What reaction do you have to the comparison between the "leap of faith" and bungee jumping or skydiving? How would you compare submitting our wills to God's will and "taking a plunge"? What risks and rewards do you see in giving God control over your life?

IF ONLY . . .

Consider *The Wizard of Oz*. Throughout the movie, Dorothy and her companions sing and dance their way toward the Emerald City, listing all the things they could do *if only*. Christians are often stalled in their journeys of faith by the same "ifs": *If only I had more money, I'd open a homeless shelter. If only I had more time, I'd get more involved.* We can become so entrenched in our own feelings of powerlessness that we don't realize what we've been capable of accomplishing all along.

At Pentecost, the Spirit was poured into young and old, male and female, slave and free. No one was exempt from sharing in the power of the Spirit. Can any aspect of human existence, then, be immune to the power of God at work in God's people? Are we really powerless to effect change in our personal relationships, health, bad habits, or finances?

Are we really unable to stand up against violence, oppression, poverty, or the bully in the office? Or can we, as empowered, Spirit-led Christians, become advocates for the poor, for peace, for justice, for the environment over which we are given dominion? The choice really is ours—*if only* we are willing to take that leap of faith.

GIVING IT UP TO GOD

Since 1935, more than 2,000,000 men and women have tackled the 12 steps of Alcoholics Anonymous in their efforts to stop drinking. Fundamental to this process is an admission of powerlessness over alcohol and a decision to turn "our will and our lives over to the care of God as we understand Him." The slogan "let go and let God" reminds them of the choice. Too often, we wait until we have exhausted every other option before calling on the Spirit's power.

A 2000 Olympic Gold Medalist, Brandon Slay, is encouraging young people to turn their lives over in a similar fashion, to "give it up to God." Slay, through his organization Greater Gold, is committed to replacing society's emphasis on wealth and winning with an emphasis on putting Christ first. The choice is ours. Do we consciously connect ourselves to God through Jesus Christ in the power of the Holy Spirit? Slay sees "giving it up" as inviting the Spirit in and allowing God to handle all those things that cause us to feel so out of control. In Christ, we have power and life. And, in the words of Brandon Slay, "Ain't it cool?"

CASE STUDIES

Getting Started

Use any of these cases in place of or in addition to the cases in the sessions as a means of stimulating discussion.

An Omnipotent God, a Suffering World

University Chapel, with its proximity to two colleges, a courthouse, and the offices of several financial and technology firms, has always boasted a thriving young adult ministry that attracts many young professionals. Bible studies, book discussion groups, work projects, and social outings are always well attended and provide a sense of community—family really—for those finishing their studies or starting their careers.

During the monthly coffeehouse, an informal potluck meal followed by "open mike" entertainment, a question began to circulate: "Has anyone seen Blair lately?" David realized that he hadn't seen her since well before Thanksgiving. Where was Blair? He couldn't remember for sure the last time he had seen her in Bible study or worship, but with three services, the holidays, and the amount of business travel among members . . . well, it was hard to keep up with everyone.

While he often found himself at odds with Blair during discussions, David did value her insights as a biomedical researcher. Her strong opinions and scientific skepticism made for some interesting, if heated, exchanges. And although they didn't socialize outside church, he decided to give her a call before Sunday.

David was surprised when Blair answered (he was ready to leave a just-checking-in message) and equally surprised by the flatness of her tone. "Hey, Blair, it's David Simms from UC. We haven't seen you for a while, and I was wondering if everything is okay." No response.

"Blair?"

"Look, David, I appreciate the call, but I'm struggling with church—with God for that matter. I flew home November 1st to watch my 32-year-old sister die. Ovarian cancer. She had a husband and two little girls. Lyn was a teacher—worked with disabled kids. Two hundred people at the funeral, and all the preacher could come up with was, 'It's not for us to understand God's plan.' Is everything okay? No. I need some space right now. I'm trying to sort things out."

Now David found himself struggling against silence. "Well, have you talked with Pastor Rivera? Maybe she—"

"No—no thanks."

—If you were David what, if anything, would you do to reach out to Blair? What would you say to Blair?

—Have you ever felt like Blair? Have any personal or world events ever caused you to question your faith? How did you come to terms with your struggles?

—Why do you think an all-powerful God allows bad things to happen to good people? What insights have you gained from Scripture to address this age-old question?

He's Got the Power

Darnell has put in more than sixty hours of unpaid, late-night overtime in the past two weeks to seal a deal that could net his company millions and himself a hefty commission. The bonus would be enough that he and his wife could secure a mortgage on a first home. In the process of preparing for the deal, he has discovered discrepancies in the firm's accounting practices.

First thing the following morning, Darnell went to his boss's office and showed him the files with the discrepancies. His boss took the file from him and began to shred the papers.

"If one word of this gets out, I'll have your head and your job."

—What power does Darnell's boss have in this situation? How would you characterize this type of power? What is its source? What power does Darnell have?

—Brainstorm a list of possible responses for Darnell. Which of these seem consistent with the "law of the jungle"? Which are consistent with the teachings of Christ?

—How would you handle the situation? What factors would contribute to your response? Would your faith come into play? How?

—Why is power so often and easily abused? How can Christians avoid the pitfalls of the power game? Can you live as a Christian in a dog-eat-dog work environment and still get ahead?

A Question of Will, a Question of Power

Kia's stomach had growled all the way through Sunday school—noticeably so. She had skipped breakfast in order to atone for yesterday's Krispy Kreme episode, but there was no way to make it through one of Reverend Bailey's sermons without a little something to tide her over. Anyway, she could start her diet on Monday—again. She headed down to coffee hour, offering up a quick prayer that Sister Lettie had baked a batch of her world-famous brownies. Besides, she was scheduled to serve as a greeter, and what better place to run into newcomers than next to the coffee pot?

As she bit into her second brownie (*Thank you, Lord!*), she noticed a well-dressed man in his late forties standing alone near the door. She waved him over to the refreshment table.

"Welcome to St. Stephen's," she said warmly. "I'm Kia, and we're so glad you're here."

"My name is Douglas."

"Well, Douglas, let me pour you some coffee, and you'll just have to try one of these fabulous brownies. As a certified chocoholic, I guarantee you've never tried one better. Are you a first-time visitor?"

"Not exactly. I've actually been coming here for several months . . . to the A.A. meetings on Tuesday night. I'm working my third step right now, trying to turn my will over to God. It's been a struggle, and I figure I could use a little help."

—What are the things that challenge your willpower? How successful have you been in tackling them on your own?

—Define *willpower*; trace this power to its source. Can God resource our willpower? Can members of the faith community help?

—What does it mean to turn one's will over to God? How might your whole life change if you were to surrender your power to God? What would you lose? What might you gain? What is holding you back?

SERVICE LEARNING OPTIONS

IDEA #1: Explore Ministries of Empowerment

"The Twelve Steps" and "The Twelve Traditions" of Alcoholics Anonymous have been adopted and adapted by other recovery programs including Narcotics Anonymous, Gamblers Anonymous, Sexual Compulsives Anonymous, and Overeaters Anonymous with great success. Countless men and women have been able to overcome addiction to destructive substances and behaviors through this process of mutual accountability and support, which begins with an admission of powerlessness and the belief that only a "power greater than ourselves could restore us to sanity."

Many of these recovery groups rely on free or low-cost meeting space that affords anonymity to those who attend. Does your church host any of these groups? Use local newspapers, Web sites, and toll free numbers for these, or similar, organizations to check for meetings in your community. Do you think such a group is needed in your area? Would your church be willing to share its facilities with those looking to "turn our will and our lives over to the care of God?"

You may want to speak to your pastor (or a parish nurse if one is available) about addressing the issue of addiction and the resources available. Collect and place brochures with contact information and local meeting times and places in an accessible location in your church. Use newsletters and handouts to share the information with your congregation.

Copies of "The Twelve Steps" and "The Twelve Traditions" are easily accessed online at the official Web sites of any of the recovery groups listed above. Read and discuss them together, noting the similarities between recovery and discipleship.

IDEA #2: Participate in a "Recharging Retreat"

Plan a weekend or a day-long time away with your class to focus on getting in touch with the Holy Spirit. Many resources for planning retreats and for discerning spiritual gifts are available through most Christian bookstores. Check with your pastor or an experienced retreat leader for assistance in finding materials and possible locations for your getaway. An established retreat or conference center will provide sleeping accommodations, meals, and meeting space. Some centers will even provide leadership for your retreat. A less expensive alternative is to plan an all-day event held in a different location. Perhaps another church would provide meeting space and low-cost meals or refreshments.

Spend time together in prayer, study, and fellowship. Use a "spiritual gifts inventory" or similar tool to discover your spiritual gifts—your "powers." Pray for empowerment from the Holy Spirit and for one another, that you may use your gifts in living out your discipleship. Make sure to allow down time, time for play and recreation, time for worship and celebration. Providing craft materials might help to get everyone's creative juices flowing.

IDEA #3: Establish a "No Bullying Zone"

In the wake of the dramatic number of school shootings across America, public and parochial school systems, denominations, and child advocacy groups have developed anti-bullying campaigns. You may want to check with professional teachers in your congregation or do an online search for "anti-bullying" to see what materials are available.

Work with your Sunday school and youth leaders, your pastor, parents, children, and youth to formulate an anti-bullying initiative in your congregation. What can the adults in your church do, through teaching and example, to help the next generation learn better ways of handling conflict? How can you help children and youth learn to use their power constructively? Work with the kids to develop a no-bullying covenant.